HISTORIC ARCHITECTURE
IN MISSISSIPPI

HISTORIC ARCHITECTURE IN MISSISSIPPI

Mary Wallace Crocker

UNIVERSITY PRESS OF MISSISSIPPI

JACKSON

Copyright © 1973 by the
University Press of Mississippi
Library of Congress Catalog Card Number 72-92483
ISBN 0-87805-022-1
Manufactured in the United States of America

Fifth Printing 1988

Contents

Preface

The purpose of this book was not to photograph every old house in Mississippi. Instead, the purpose was to select representative historic buildings from various sections of the state. A building can be referred to as "historic" for several reasons: (1) a notable person occupied or is associated with the house; (2) an important event is related to the structure; (3) the building is historically significant because of its design; (4) the building is recognized for its construction.

Initially the Historic American Buildings Survey was used as a reference in locating the houses, but it was found to be inadequate for a statewide study since Holly Springs, Oxford, and other areas with many fine buildings were omitted from the listing. In addition to the HABS, the Federal Writers Project for Mississippi was consulted, and the chambers of commerce and historical societies in the towns were contacted. After a master list was developed, the researcher wrote to the homeowners for appointments to see the houses and to interview people who were familiar with the histories of the buildings. After visits and interviews, photographs were made of selected structures. Further research was undertaken in the local and state libraries.

The writer did not attempt to verify the dates for the houses. Most of the dates were checked by either the homeowner or a local historian when many of the pilgrimages were initiated.

An effort was made to determine the name and occupation of the builder, to ascertain whether an architect or design book was consulted for the design of the house, to classify the style of architecture, to note alterations made in the structures, and to list any folktales or legends associated with the house. In photographing the buildings special emphasis was given to rear views of the houses, outbuildings, and outstanding interior features such as millwork, stairways, mantels, and decorative plasterwork. There are many photographs of the facades of Mississippi buildings, but photos of details are almost non-existent. The photographs for this publication were taken to show as much of the building as possible. They were made to illustrate, not to dramatize.

Another purpose of the book was to stimulate interest in the history of important buildings in Mississippi. The compilation of known facts concerning the buildings may be helpful to graduate students and historical societies in identifying gaps and recognizing topics that need to be researched.

To locate historic buildings in Mississippi, to photograph them, to find relevant references and to write about the structures could be a lifetime project. This book, however, was prepared in four years because the author considered time to be an important factor as houses are destroyed routinely by man and nature, and people who know about the structures die. Although this manuscript may not be as comprehensive as some people would like, it is the most complete study attempted so far.

Hopefully, the book is free of errors — that, of course, would be a rarity for a historical manuscript. If readers should discover a mistake or would like a point clarified in later editions, please write to the author in care of the publisher.

To prepare a book of this type requires the cooperation of many people. First, I would like to acknowledge my husband, Jack, who helped edit the manuscript and offered suggestions and encouragement through the years. Thanks also go to my family and friends who were very patient with me while I devoted many hours to this project. The homeowners were most cooperative. The words "Mississippi hospitality" have a new meaning to me after having visited the homes of these gracious people (homeowners are listed in the appendix). Librarians throughout the state were helpful as I searched for information on the Mississippi buildings. Special thanks go to Miss Dawn Mattox and Mr. Ron Miller, architectural historians with the Department of Archives and History in Jackson and to the library staff at Mississippi State College for Women — especially Mrs. Patsy McDaniel who processed my interlibrary loan requests. I would also like to express my gratitude to Miss Amanda Harris, Miss Brenda Jones, and Mrs. Virginia Hunter who helped in the preparation of the manuscript.

Mary Wallace Crocker

Columbus, Mississippi
April, 1973

Introduction

Mississippi, a state since 1817, has a good representation of different styles of historic architecture. The styles — Spanish Provincial, Classic Revival, Romantic Revival, Italianate, Oriental Revival, and Octagonal form — correspond with those built elsewhere in the United States but were adapted to fit the local climate, geography, native material supply, and political and socioeconomic conditions. Each of these factors will be considered briefly.

Climate. The climate in Mississippi is best described as moderate, with the absence of extreme temperatures. Snow occurs rarely so there is no need for steep roofs. Chimneys were necessary as fireplaces were used for heating the houses. The design of the chimney was influenced by the prevailing style. Since Greek temples did not have chimneys, houses built during the Greek Revival period had chimneys that were recessed and had a plain stack so that they would be inconspicuous.

Galleries were popular on Mississippi houses. Double or single galleries were frequently used across the front and back of the house and occasionally a house would have a gallery encircling the main structure. The porches not only shaded the walls of the house but also provided a place to sit and hope for a breeze. With the protection of a porch the windows and doors could be left open in rainy weather.

Many houses had floor-length windows that opened onto the galleries. The windows might be tall windows that opened to the floor, or a double hung window with the wall underneath designed to open to make a doorway. The convertible door-window is known as a jib door.

Often the low roofs were topped with a cupola that not only served as an observatory but also provided light for the central hallways. In addition, when the windows in the cupola (often twelve to sixteen) were opened, a natural draft was created for the hot air to rise and pass through the cupola windows.

Raised cottages with the main level on the second floor were popular, especially in southern Mississippi. By having the house some distance from the ground, air could pass under the floors to cool them. Also many people associated yellow fever with the soil; therefore they considered the air at the upper level to be more healthful.

The walls in some of the houses measure as much as twenty-six inches in thickness. If the shutters on the windows were closed at the appropriate times to keep the sun from penetrating the house, the air inside the massive walls was kept cool.

Geography. There is a close relationship between the location of the houses and the rivers and the soil types (see maps). The main river, of course, was the Mississippi, which is the western boundary for the state. Residents of houses in the Delta, Vicksburg, Port Gibson, Natchez, and Fort Adams could export and import goods and travel the mighty

Territorial Rivers and Roads. Used by permission of Steck-Vaughn Company.

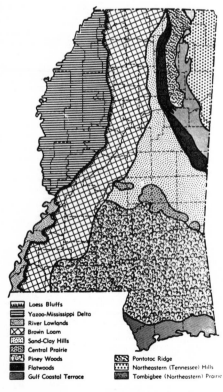

Mississippi Soil Areas. Used by permission of Steck-Vaughn Company.

river. On the eastern side of the state the Tombigbee flowed down to Mobile, Alabama, to empty into the Gulf. This river meant that residents of Aberdeen, Columbus, and Macon could export and import supplies easily. Jackson and the John Ford house are near the Pearl River, while Pascagoula homes line the Pascagoula "Singing River." Many creeks and bayous are located throughout the state.

Most of the early houses are located in areas where the soil is especially fertile, since farming was the major source of income. A wide ribbon of brown loam soil curves from the southwestern part of the state up to the north central section. This fertile area did not extend to the city of Natchez but it was a part of the region known in earlier years as Natchez. However, many of the Natchezians chose to live on the bluffs of the Natchez township while they farmed lands in the Louisiana Delta. Another important region for cotton, and ultimately mansions, was the Tombigbee Prairie where the towns of Aberdeen, Columbus and Macon developed.

Although acres of fertile land existed in the Mississippi Delta, this region was sparsely settled because of the devastating floods that occurred when the Mississippi River overflowed. After levees were constructed in the 1850s some important houses were constructed.

Native Materials. Wood as a building material was readily available since oak and pine trees grow in most areas of Mississippi. In the southern part of the state the cypress tree is also plentiful. Often the millwork and floors in southern houses are of cypress.

The clay-sand soil was easily obtainable for making good bricks. A number of the early Spanish houses in Natchez are brick on the first level, with brick floors, while the upper level is of wood. Springfield, a red brick mansion built in 1791 by Thomas M. Green of Georgia, was one of the first solid brick houses to be built in Mississippi.

Brick was a popular building material in Holly Springs also, where even today fine bricks are still being made. Numerous Holly Springs houses have solid brick walls which extend to the ground. An iron foundry was an early industry in Holly Springs, which no doubt accounts for the fact that many of the houses are ornamented with lovely iron balconies, window cornices and capitals, and are enclosed with iron fences.

When money became plentiful, a common practice for house builders was to import slate for roofs, mantels of marble, side and transom lights of stained and etched glass, and carved wood for millwork. Many of the furnishings were also imported.

Political and Socioeconomic Influences. Early Mississippi history revolved around the Natchez area. Located on the bluffs of the Mississippi River with many creeks and bayous feeding the fertile land of the Mississippi territory and the Louisiana Delta, Natchez, known for its natural beauty, became important first as a fort built by the French, then as a port developed by the British and Spanish, then as a cotton farming region. For ten years the Natchez region had a Spanish governor, English-speaking Don Gayoso, who earned the respect of many people regardless of their nationalities. Gayoso and his staff built comfortable homes and developed a city plan for the town of Natchez. See the Natchez section for a description of the Spanish influences.

The Natchez area became important from the standpoint of economics when the production of cotton became prevalent. After Eli Whitney invented the cotton gin in 1794 and Dr. Rush Nutt improved the variety of Mexican cotton seed, cotton became known as white gold. Many professional men turned to farming because it was so profitable. The affluence was reflected in the homes that were constructed. Planters sought architects or master builders with good design books to build stately mansions. By 1812 the Classic style of architecture had definitely arrived when Levi Weeks, an architect from Massachusetts, built the beautiful mansion known as Auburn for Lyman Harding. The white-pillared rage was to continue until the 1860s.

After the Choctaw and Chickasaw Indians ceded their lands to the United States in the 1830s, the towns known as Columbus, Carrollton, Aberdeen, Macon, Oxford, Pontotoc, and Holly Springs began to develop. Again, cotton was the main crop. Mansions were built in these towns from the 1840s to the 1860s.

Most of the big houses followed the same floor plan regardless of the size of the family or the occupation of the builder. Central hallways divided the eight-room, two-story houses equally. Most of the houses had a parlor or double parlors, dining room, and a guest bedroom on the lower level. Since entertaining in the home rather than in public places predominated during this era, sliding doors, folding doors, and jib doors were often incorporated into the design of the lower level so that one side of the house or the whole downstairs area could be opened to accommodate large parties and balls. The second story was reserved for sleeping apartments.

The kitchen was usually detached from the main house since cooking on an open fireplace was considered hazardous. Furthermore, having food odors inside the big house was objectionable. Sometimes a covered walkway joined the kitchen to the main house.

The kitchens in areas other than Natchez were usually small, very plain, brick buildings. In Natchez, however, many of the houses had two, 2-story brick dependencies behind the main house. These dependencies were one room deep with each room opening onto a long gallery (see photo of Concord quarters). The kitchen and storage rooms were on the lower levels while the servants' quarters were on the upper levels.

Other special purpose buildings behind some of the big houses included a privy, a garcons' room, a billiard room, a school room, a dairy house (for cooling dairy products), a smokehouse (for curing meat), a carriagehouse, and stables.

Maintaining the big house and its entourage of buildings did not present many problems for the owner since he usually was wealthy enough to own servants to do the work.

Source of Designs. More research needs to be done to determine the designers and sources for designs of many of the Mississippi buildings. The following is a list of architects' names who have been associated with buildings in the state: Natchez — Juan Scott, Levi Weeks, James Griffen, James Hardie, Samuel Sloan; Jackson — William Nichols; Raymond and Vicksburg — Weldon Brothers; Columbus — James Lull and William O'Neal; Oxford — William Nichols, Calvert Vaux; Carrollton — James Clark Harris; Canton and Annandale — Frank Wills; Ocean Springs — Louis Sullivan and Frank Lloyd Wright; Aberdeen — Daniel H. Burnham. Most of the houses were probably built by carpenters who relied on design books and the instructions of the house owner for direction.

The design of Dr. Haller Nutt's Longwood in Natchez appeared in Samuel Sloan's *The Model Architect* in 1852. After the plan was adapted by Sloan to fit Nutt's specifications, the plan appeared in Sloan's *Homestead Architecture* in 1861. Craftsmen from Philadelphia constructed Longwood. The facade of Ammadelle in Oxford follows design number twenty-seven in Calvert Vaux's book *Villas and Cottages* (1857). The owner has the original plans for the house. The plans have Vaux's name printed on each sheet. The interior millwork details of the Governor's Mansion in Jackson and Stanton Hall in Natchez appear very similar to plates in Minard Lefever's *Modern Builder's Guide*. The Manship house in Jackson resembles Figure 128 in Andrew Downing's *The Architecture of Country Houses*. The influence of Orson Fowler can be seen in Mon Amour at Horn Lake. The house has the same floor plan as the Howland plan in Fowler's book, *A Home for All,* published in 1854. Further research would probably make this list longer.

Styles. The Spanish Provincial style predominates among the territorial houses in Mississippi. Most of these houses are in Natchez and date to the 1790s. The houses fall into three categories: (1) the long narrow house with front and back galleries, i.e., Airlie, The Gardens; (2) the two-story house that is brick on the lower level, wood on the upper, with double galleries and a canted roof, i.e., Concord, Connelly's Tavern, Saragossa; (3) solid brick, square structures located close to the streets, i.e., Texada, Conti, and Lawyer's Row. The Spanish House at Biloxi would fit into the third category.

The Classic style with much adaptation predominates in antebellum houses of Mississippi. Many of the mansions in Natchez have round columns with Tuscan or Doric capitals, fanlighted doorways, keystone windows, and looped staircases in recessed halls. Around 1840 the doorway treatment changed from the fanlight to the horizontal transom with sidelights. This arrangement was used consistently in other parts of Mississippi. The backs of the Natchez houses are frequently as attractive as the facades.

In Columbus the square, paneled pillars were more popular than round columns. Also there were many flat or low roofs capped with a cupola or a captain's walk. The sidelights around the doors are often of colored glass while beautiful plasterwork incorporating Greek motifs adorn the interior ceilings. Riverview and Waverley probably have the finest plasterwork in the state. These same two houses contain spectacular stairwells (see Columbus section for photos).

Holly Springs has the most decorated Greek Revival houses (excepting Natchez' Stanton Hall) with Corinthian capitals, decorative window cornices, and iron grillwork outlining the balconies and porches. Curved stairways predominate in Holly Springs.

Italianate houses are well represented in the state by Rosedale and White Arches in Columbus, Ammadelle in Oxford and Mount Holly near

Lake Washington. Rounded-arch windows, bracketed eaves, grillwork, and low roofs are characteristics found in these houses. Both of the Columbus houses have towers.

Holly Springs claims the best Gothic houses in the state with Cedarhurst and Airliewood. These houses are very similar, with high pitched roofs and gables embellished with fanciful bargeboards and decorative finials and pendants. The pointed arch, a characteristic motif of Gothic buildings, is achieved in Cedarhurst by shaped bricks; whereas hoods or labels are used on Airliewood. Both buildings have tall, paired, octagonal chimneys.

Sometimes as the popularity of one style waned and another gained momentum, the old and the new were brought together. Such was the case in Mississippi during the late 1850s when both the Greek and Gothic motifs were incorporated into the same building. This was done very effectively in Columbus in the houses Shadowlawn, Errolton, and Themerlaine. In Holly Springs, a unique structure was formed when octagonal towers were combined with a classic portico at Walter Place.

In the 1850s Orson Fowler promoted the use of the octagonal form as the most "logical form" for houses. A house built according to a plan in Fowler's design book is at Horn Lake, Mississippi. Other octagonal houses in the state are Longwood in Natchez and one of the Sullivan cottages at Ocean Springs. The Governor's Mansion has an octagonal entrance hall; Waverley (near Columbus) and Snowdoun (Columbus) have octagonal stairwells surmounted by octagonal cupolas — the cupola on Snowdoun has been removed; White Arches (Columbus) has an octagonal tower; and Walter Place (Holly Springs) has two octagonal towers. The interior of the sanctuary of the First Methodist Church in Aberdeen is octagonal. Senator J. Z. George's law library at Carrollton is hexagonal.

The Oriental style can be seen in the unfinished thirty-two room, octagonal mansion named Longwood in Natchez. According to its architect Samuel Sloan, the Moorish arches and the bulbiform dome qualify this building to be labeled oriental.

The shingle style, for which McKim, Mead, and White were especially noted, was popular in the latter part of the nineteenth century. This style is represented in Mississippi by three houses in Ocean Springs; these houses were constructed for Louis Sullivan, the famous Chicago architect. According to Sullivan's biographer,[1] the bungalows were designed by Sullivan. However, Frank Lloyd Wright, who was working as a draftsman for Sullivan at the time the buildings were constructed, wrote that he designed the buildings.[2] Either way, the buildings were designed by a famous architect to be used as summer homes for Louis Sullivan and his friends.

Many of the houses in this book do not necessarily fit into any style category. These houses may be important because of the uniqueness of the design, the way they are constructed, or because some historic event or a well-known person is associated with the house.

NOTES TO INTRODUCTION

[1] Hugh Morrison, *Louis Sullivan* (New York: W. W. Norton & Co., 1935), p. 112.
[2] Frank Lloyd Wright, *Genius and the Mobocracy* (New York: Horizon Press, 1971), p. 67.

Natchez and Vicinity

For many people the word Natchez is synonymous with stately mansions. D'Evereux, Dunleith, Melrose, and Stanton Hall are examples of such mansions and are surely among the most photographed houses in America. In addition to the luxurious mansions that were built during the King Cotton era, Natchez also has many examples of architecture that date to the time when the town was ruled by a Spanish governor (1779–1798); and there are possibly three buildings that were constructed during the British period (1763–1779).

KING'S TAVERN

King's Tavern is generally considered to be of English origin and also to be the oldest structure in Natchez, although the exact date of the building is not known. However, heavy beams, wooden pegs, low

King's Tavern

ceilings, barred windows, and the condition of the timbers help to indicate the approximate age of the structure. The three-story building fronts the present-day sidewalk and is constructed of brick on the first level and cypress and poplar on the upper levels. Some of the building materials appear to have come from a dismantled ship. Since lumber mills were nonexistent at this early date, prepared lumber from boats was certainly sought after. The restoration of King's Tavern is an admirable project undertaken by the Pilgrimage Garden Club.

HOPE FARM

Hope Farm is divided into two distinct buildings. The rear structure is regarded by some historians as English, dating from 1775 (Photo). It is a two-story, double-gallery structure with low ceilings and fine millwork (Photo).

The front section of the house is Spanish and probably was erected around 1789 by Carlos de Grand Pre, a Spanish governor. The house, with its broad, sloping roof and long gallery, is constructed of heavy

Hope Farm — rear section

Hope Farm — interior, rear section

Hope Farm — Spanish section

timbers held together by tongue-and-groove and wooden-pin techniques. In 1830 changes were made to form a double parlor in the front of the house.

The beauty of the architecture is greatly enhanced by the spacious, old-fashioned garden and rear patio as well as its appropriate antique furnishings. Hope Farm is the home of Katherine Grafton Miller, the originator of the Natchez pilgrimage, and her husband Mr. J. Balfour Miller.

Mt. Locust

MT. LOCUST

Located on the Natchez Trace, approximately sixteen miles from Natchez, is another English structure of the pioneer type. This structure was probably built by a retired British naval officer named Blommart shortly after Natchez was surrendered from England to Spain. After a couple of years the house was sold to William Ferguson, a Virginian, who enlarged it into an inn for Natchez Trace travelers. The National Park Service has restored Mt. Locust to appear as it did in the 1820s. The house is open to the public.

Spanish houses other than the front section of Hope Farm are: Airlie, The Gardens, Connelly's Tavern, Saragossa, rear wing of Evansview, The Elms, and sections of other houses that have been vastly remodeled or enlarged (Cottage Gardens, Cherokee, Holly Hedges). Concord, home of the Spanish governor Gayoso, burned. Most of the houses have some or all of the following features: built on two levels, with the first level usually constructed of brick, and the upper level of wood; brick floors on the first level, wood on the upper level; small fenestrations with slender frames and wooden louvered shutters; galleries that span the length of the house supported by slender columns; a lower level frequently designed for passage of a carriage through the house; a roof that is usually canted or gently sloped; and a rear patio with cistern for water.

Texada, Conti, and Lawyers' Row represent another type of Spanish house. Rather than long and narrow, they are block-like structures, located close to the street, are constructed with thick brick walls, and have small windows with shutters.

EVANSVIEW

Evansview, an L-shaped structure known earlier as Bontura, is interesting because of its architecture, landscaping, and location. The house is located on the bluffs above the Mississippi River at the head of the entrance to Silver Street and Natchez-under-the-hill, which was

Natchez under the Hill

Evansview

Evansview — brick detail

the business area of early Natchez. Many of the early buildings have been claimed by the river, and the few that remain are in a deteriorated condition. Natchez-under-the-hill activities have been vividly described in a publication of the same name by Mrs. Edith Wyatt Moore. The park area in front of Evansview parallels the Mississippi River. With its grand view of the river, this park has been important throughout the history of Natchez as a parade ground for the military and a lovely area for promenades (a favorite pastime of the Spaniards, especially on Sundays and holidays).

Evansview, like many of the Spanish houses, has undergone changes through the years. Often the houses were enlarged by adding wings to the Spanish section or by incorporating the older house within the framework of a new structure. Therefore, in discussing Spanish architecture, the reference may be to a part, or section, of a house rather than to the whole structure. This is true for Evansview; the back wings are the Spanish section, while the more decorative front section was added during the early nineteenth century.

The rear wings are two stories high and only one room deep, with the double galleries supported by slender posts. The brick detail (Photo) of the arches in the short part of the L-structure is especially attractive. The arches are tall enough so that carriages could drive underneath. The rear wings are fronted with brick walks and a garden that contains an old cistern and native flowers. Green latticework is used between the posts on the upper gallery to shield the rooms from the evening sun.

The front section of Evansview is distinctive because of the decorative iron grillwork and the asymmetrical plan. Entry is into a small hall and the parlor is located to the right. Behind the parlor and separated by folding doors is a room that spans the width of the house and has a fireplace at each end. A window in this room faces the courtyard, while a rear door opens onto the brick paved gallery. Access to the second floor is by a small staircase in the foyer that leads to an upper hall and two bedrooms over the front section. An outside stairway leads to the rooms in the wings. Another stair leads to the attic, which is lighted by a dormer window. This floor plan is typical of town house plans that were popular in New Orleans, Mobile, and along the East Coast.

The house was purchased in 1860 by Don Jose Bontura, a business-man from Portugal who had a tavern in old Natchez-under-the-hill. The Bonturas probably entertained many persons associated with river-boat history. In 1941 the house was acquired and restored by Mr. and Mrs. Hugh Evans of Los Angeles, who later gave it and its elegant furnishings to the National Society of the Colonial Dames of America in the State of Mississippi.

CONNELLY'S TAVERN

Connelly's Tavern, located two blocks north of Evansview, also overlooks the esplanade, or parade ground, and the Mississippi River from its lofty site on Ellicott's Hill (where Andrew Elliott raised the American flag in 1797). This two-story building with an attractive canted roof and double galleries has served as a residence, a tavern, a site for entertaining royalty (the Duke of Orleans, who was later King Louis Philippe of France), a school, and since 1935 as a national shrine and headquarters for the Natchez Garden Club.

The exact date of construction of Connelly's Tavern is not known. However, in 1795 the spot known then as Gilreath's Hill was granted by the Spanish government to Solomon Sweazie. In 1797 when the property passed from Sweazie to Patrick Connelly, the deed indicated "houses, outhouses, buildings, hereditaments and appurtenances what-soever." Therefore, the erection of the tavern seems to have been between the years 1795 and 1797.

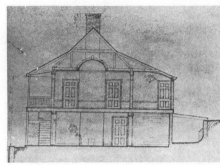

Connelly's Tavern—cross section shows arched ceiling and drawbridge (HABS)

Connelly's Tavern—gable on hip roof

The design of Connelly's Tavern contains several unique features. For example, a safety precaution incorporated was a moat that parallels the back of the house. Drawbridges could be released for passage from the second floor to the hill behind the house (Photo). Although raw building materials were abundant during this period, they were time-consuming to prepare for construction. Consequently, materials from flatboats and shipping vessels were used whenever possible. This practice may explain why some of the ceilings in Connelly's Tavern are arched. The first floor of the building has low ceilings, brick floors, and simple fireplaces. This level was used for the tavern and kitchen. The upper floor was the residence and contains finer architectural features.

SARAGOSSA

The canted roof and wide eaves of Saragossa are similar to those of Connelly's Tavern. However, the general appearance of Saragossa is much more provincial, with its brick pillars on the lower level and sturdy wooden pillars on the upper contrasting sharply with the slender colonettes of Connelly's Tavern. Also, instead of a wooden balustrade, a heavy chain is used between the wood columns. Suffice it to say that Saragossa is almost fortresslike in appearance with its ruggedness and simplicity constituting its beauty. The natural setting of yucca, live oak trees, and moss is in complete harmony with the building. Saragossa has been the home for five generations of the Smith family.

AIRLIE

Airlie and Cottage Gardens were both probably built by Don Jose Vidal, a Castillian officer. Airlie, located on a wooded knoll, is approached by a circular drive. Decorative iron posts are located on each side of the broad steps that lead to the spacious gallery. Through the years additions have been made to the early structure, but the horizontal emphasis and general Spanish Provincial feeling have been maintained. The small windows and doors can be covered with louvered wooden shutters that give privacy and protection from the sun, yet allow ventilation. The upper sections of the double doors at the entry are louvered. The doors open into a central hallway that separates long, spacious rooms that have other doors opening onto the gallery. Since

Saragossa

Airlie

Airlie is one of the oldest structures in Natchez it is not surprising to see hand-hewn timbers with the beams held together with pegs.

Airlie is occupied by descendants of the Ayres P. Merrill family, who moved to Airlie from Elms Court. Mr. Merrill married a daughter of Frank Surget, one of Natchez' first millionaires. During U. S. Grant's administration, Mr. Merrill was named minister to Belgium. Much of the fine furniture that belonged to this family is now in Airlie.

THE GARDENS

Similar in design to Airlie, The Gardens is a long, narrow building with a sloping roof, slender columns, and a gallery that spans the width of the house. The house has many fenestrations that open onto the gallery. Small formal gardens are laid out on top of the bluff in front of the house; hence the name, The Gardens. The house is known locally as the home of Louisa Pyrnelle, who wrote the children's story, *Diddie, Dumps and Tot* which was published in 1882.

The Gardens

The intersection at Wall and Washington streets has a house on each corner that possesses some Spanish construction. These houses are described below.

TEXADA

Texada is one of the largest and most typical of the boxlike Spanish houses, with a very plain exterior, brick walls rising from the sidewalk, and small windows with shutters for privacy and protection from the sun. The property dates back to a 1792 land grant to Miguel Sobbellas. Mr. Maurice Stockpole bought the house at public auction and sold it one month later to Don Miguel Garcia de Texada, a tavernkeeper, landowner, and slaveholder who arrived in Natchez about 1781.

Texada has been used as a residence, a tavern, a meeting place for the Territorial legislature, an antique shop, and recently restored once

Texada — service quarters

Texada

Holly Hedge

Leisure House

again for a residence by Dr. and Mrs. George W. Moss. Historians, architects, and the population in general should be delighted that this Spanish-American edifice was preserved. A two-story, four-room servants' quarters is located behind the big house (Photo).

HOLLY HEDGES

Holly Hedges, located to the left of Texada, was restored by Earl Hart Miller and his wife. The original deed for Holly Hedges is written in Spanish and lists Don Juan Scott as the builder in 1796. This reference is to the central basement part of the house with its tile floors and original cistern. According to D. Clayton James, Don Juan Scott was a Scotsman who is referred to in the Spanish archives as a shipwright, a markethouse operator, carpenter, and physician, as well as architect.[1]

The house was purchased in 1818 by Judge Edward Turner who gave the property to his daughter when she married John T. McMurran. The McMurrans enlarged the house and added the lovely fanlighted doorway and dormer windows with interlacing arched panes. The McMurrans later built stately Melrose.

Across from Holly Hedges and Texada are the Leisure House and Dixie. The Leisure House (301 South Wall Street) was probably constructed around 1794 by Hugh Coyle, a tailor. Other owners were Jose Texada (brother of Don Texada), John Griffith (attorney who founded the State Bar Association in Mississippi), and Anna Willis McComas (a relative of George Washington). The house has been used as a parsonage for the First Baptist Church and is presently a residence-bookstore. The house has a canted roof, double galleries with slender colonnettes both front and rear, and an outside stairway. Typically, the lower level is brick, while the upper is of timber. The fanlighted front door is a later addition.

The rear wing of Dixie possibly dates to the Spanish occupation. The front part of the house was built for Samuel Davis, older brother of Jefferson Davis.

THE ELMS

Six blocks east of the Washington and Wall intersection is located a fine Spanish Provincial house known as The Elms. Without the galleries and decorative balustrades, the house would be at home on most any street in Spain. The thick, stuccoed walls; low ceilings; small fenestrations with shutters attached by iron hinges; and the brick patios—all bespeak of its early heritage.

The building consists of three stories, with four rooms and a hall on the first two levels and two large rooms on the third level. Before additions were made, the galleries surrounded the house and were connected by a decorative iron stair, which has now been enclosed within a corridor. The Elms has always been surrounded by spacious grounds featuring gardens in formal designs. Octagonal summer houses, three cisterns, a billiard room, and a carriage house were once part of The Elms assemblage. The earliest record regarding this property refers to William Barland, who obtained a Spanish land grant in 1782.

The Elms

LINDEN

Linden is a simple, elegant building whose central portion may date to the late 1780s. The cypress timbers in the building are held together with wooden pegs. The central floorplan consists of two rooms and a hall on two levels. When the building was acquired by Mr. Thomas B. Reed (who became attorney general of Mississippi and then a United States senator), he enlarged the building by adding wings to each side of the house, thus making the front gallery ninety-eight feet long. A

Linden

second-story portico of excellent dimensions relieves the horizontal emphasis that is created by the long gallery. The exquisite fanlighted doorway with side lights and pilasters was probably added at this time also.

Other owners of Linden include Dr. John Ker, who purchased the house from Reed's widow. Dr. Ker was a medical doctor, a planter, and a senator. In 1840 the house was purchased by Jane Gustine Conner, widow of Dr. William C. Conner. Mrs. Conner had the two dependencies constructed behind the house, thus forming an attractive courtyard while providing additional space for her family. The house is still occupied by descendants of this family.

WIGWAM

Like Linden, the central portion of the Wigwam probably dates to the late eighteenth century. The spacious side rooms presumably were added when the Wigwam became the first home of Mr. and Mrs. Douglas L. Rivers. Mrs. Rivers was the niece of Mr. and Mrs. Peter Little of Rosalie, who reared her.

The house has several interesting features. A flying-wing stairway dominates the attractive entrance hall that is further embellished with plaster cornices, plaster ceiling ornaments, and arched and paneled doors. A large room on the left side of the house is referred to as the ballroom. The walls and ceiling reportedly were painted by Dominique Canova (Photo: Detail of ceiling).

Wigwam

Wigwam — ceiling detail attributed to Dominique Canova

Thomas H. Gandy

Concord

CONCORD

The most well-known Spanish house in the Natchez region (destroyed by fire in 1900) was the residence of Don Manuel Gayoso de Lemos, governor of the region from 1789 to 1797. The house was known not only for its luxuriousness but also for the hospitality of its owner.

Gayoso was born in Lisbon, where his father was Spanish consul in the Portuguese port. Gayoso was educated in England and served the king of Spain in several posts before being selected as governor of the Natchez region in America. While in Spain he learned how to entertain lavishly, and this skill became very much a part of Gayoso's way of life whether he was in Spain, New Orleans, or Natchez. Research by Jack D. L. Holmes has revealed that Gayoso often entertained beyond his means. In 1791, Gayoso wrote to Esteban Miro, his immediate superior in New Orleans, "I have earned the affection of these people, using all my power having entertained and dined them all of which I do to the sacrifice of my own interests to the point of going into debt."[2]

When Gayoso arrived in Natchez there was no governor's mansion awaiting him. However, Commandant Carlos de Grand-Pre had written in 1788 to proper authorities to inform them that there was no suitable residence for the commandant of Natchez. He was instructed to rent a house until a new structure, that should not exceed $8,000, could be built.[3] Gayoso named the new governor's mansion Concord.

Like the other Spanish structures in Natchez, the first level of Concord was brick, while the upper levels were of wood. The lower level had an opening in the center for the carriages to pass through. The canted roof covered galleries that surrounded the house. The edifice was altered in later years by the addition of a classic portico and Tuscan

Concord — service quarters

columns. This was probably done by Stephen Minor[4] who bought Concord in 1800 for $10,000.[5] Minor, who came from Virginia, served as adjutant of the Natchez Post. He was named commandant of the Natchez region in 1797 when Gayoso became governor general of Louisiana.[6]

Concord was occupied by the Minor family until 1867.[7] A fire destroyed the house in 1900 leaving only a brick dependency and curved stairs with an iron rail. The steps were later dismantled because they were considered to be a safety hazard. The dependency still exists and is similar to others in Natchez (Photo).

SPRINGFIELD

Located near Coles Creek and the Natchez Trace is the plantation home built by Thomas M. Green, Jr., around 1791. Green came to Natchez from Georgia where his father had been instrumental in having the Natchez region temporarily included in Bourbon County of Georgia in 1785. Mr. Green was a successful cotton planter and was active in territorial politics after the Spaniards evacuated the Natchez region. His brother, Abner Green, was territorial treasurer of Mississippi while his brother-in-law, Cato West, was acting governor of the territory from 1803 to 1805.

Another well-known name associated with Springfield is that of Andrew Jackson. According to tradition, the wedding of Jackson and Rachel Donelson Robards occurred in the red-brick mansion during its first summer. Colonel Green performed the ceremony.

Springfield is one of the largest and most elaborate of the early houses in Mississippi. The house is approximately sixty-eight feet long by fifty-six feet wide, with the wall thicknesses ranging from twenty to twenty-six inches. The photo of the entrance hall shows the interior wall thickness, the dado, and the cornice gougework.

Tuscan columns, double galleries, and a formal arrangement of small

Springfield — paneled millwork and ornate cornice

Springfield — corner fireplace

Springfield

Christ Church

fenestrations predominate in the facade detail. The double doors at the entry are mounted with wrought-iron, butterfly hinges, while the sidelights in this early house are detached.

The interior millwork is especially interesting; the mantels and cornices are decorated with reeding and gougework patterns. The wainscoting, doors, and doorframes are paneled. One of the bedrooms contains a corner fireplace.

Because of the early construction of this house, wooden pegs and mortise-and-tenon methods of assembly were employed.

CHRIST CHURCH

Not far from Springfield is the community known as Church Hill, an appropriate name since many of the rolling hills are topped with small churches. Its most outstanding structure is the little Gothic chapel located on a terraced hill.

MISTLETOE

John Bisland, a Scotsman, settled in Natchez as early as 1770 and accumulated vast acreage through grants and purchases. Although the Bisland homeplace was destroyed by fire, there remain three houses on the Bisland property that are especially noteworthy. Family papers reveal that the house known as Mistletoe was built in 1807 by John Bisland for his son Peter (nineteen), who had just married Barbara Foster (sixteen). The honeymoon cottage has one and one-half stories, with the upper level unfinished. The floor plan contains four rooms divided by a central hallway. Entry is through slender double doors spanned by a fanlight. The sidelights combine square and rectangular panes of old glass that can be covered by interior shutters.

In contrast to the many long, narrow buildings of the Spaniards and the luxurious mansions that were soon to follow, the simple style and scale of Mistletoe make it an architectural prize. In general, the beauty of Mistletoe lies in its emphasis on construction materials rather than added decoration. For example, entry is over a cherry-log threshold into a hallway with wooden walls painted a delicate green, a popular color during the Federal period in the United States—the

Mistletoe

period in which the house was constructed. The floors throughout are natural cypress, as are the walls in the sitting room to the left of the hallway. This room has an air of informality with its horizontally sheathed natural cypress walls and a large fireplace that is located off center. Actually the fireplace with its exquisitely carved wood mantel is in the right-hand outer corner of the wall. Beautiful millwork surrounds the 56-inch-wide windows and the 138-inch-tall doors.

A small room presently used as a library is located behind the sitting room. This room lacks a fireplace. There is speculation that the big fireplace in the front room is in the corner so that some heat would "spill over" into the back room.

To the right of the central hallway is a guest bedroom. This room, like all the others, is exquisitely furnished in a comfortable, eclectic fashion. The house is filled with treasures inherited and collected by the S. H. Lambdins.

The back porch was enclosed with shutters and contains a small staircase that gives access to the attic. The cottage has been enlarged twice, with each addition contributing to the beauty of the original structure. Sometime after 1847 a large dining room was added to the left side of the building, and a long gallery was built across the back of the house. To make the house more functional for twentieth-century living, the Lambdins added the present-day kitchen and bedroom wings, incorporating materials obtained from original plantation buildings.[8] These wings form a U-shaped courtyard that is landscaped on two levels and includes the old brick cistern. Clipped jasmine and seasonal flowers make this area a constant scene of beauty.

MOUNT REPOSE

Near Mistletoe is a house named Mount Repose that was built by William Bisland around 1824. The large, wood-frame structure has double galleries and fanlighted doorways. Ownership of Mount Repose has remained within the family of the builder. Some of the letters that were written to John Bisland by his sons while they were in school in Glasgow, as well as other family papers and furnishings, are housed in Mount Repose. A daughter of William Bisland had the elegant mansion Edgewood built on nearby Bisland property. This house will be described later.

Mount Repose

GLOUCESTER

Gloucester is truly a historic house, significant not only for its architecture but also because it was the home of Mississippi's first

Gloucester

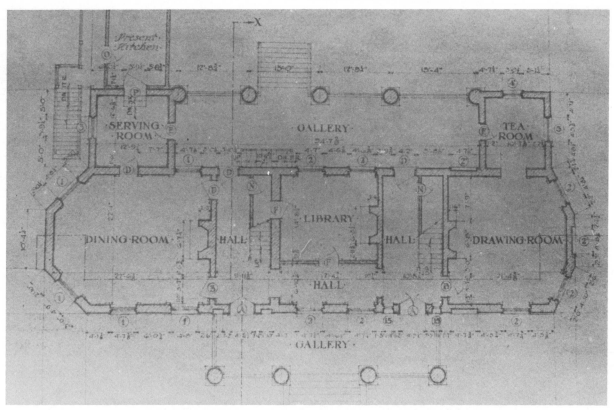

Gloucester — floor plan (HABS)

Gloucester — kitchen interior

Gloucester — kitchen and service building

territorial governor. The house was probably built around 1800 by John Scott for David Williams. The classic front was added around 1808 following the designs of Levi Weeks, an architect from Boston.[9]

A glance at the exterior of the large, red-brick structure is enough to detect that the house is unusual. The building is octagonal rather than rectangular (see floor plan). Like the Spanish houses, this house is only one room deep, with galleries across the front and back. Also, there are two main entries, with deeply recessed doorways with fanlights. The paneled recessed area gives some indication of the wall thickness. The doors are similar to the ones Levi Weeks designed for Jefferson Military College. Notice that the sidelights accompany the doorway but, at this early date, are not a part of the doorway detail. A feature that cannot be seen in the photograph because of the landscaping is a bricked areaway that fronts the basement. In earlier years this area was outlined by an iron fence.

To the left of the house are two large brick buildings and a cistern. The kitchen was located in the section with the opened door (Photo). The kitchen has a large fireplace, and is furnished with utensils of yesteryear (Photo). Note the wooden strip for hanging utensils. A built-in oven and shelves are to the right of the fireplace. The stairway on the outside of the building leads to the servants' quarters. The other building contained the billiard room and bedrooms on the upper level for the young men of the family.

In 1808 Gloucester with its dependencies and surrounding acreage was purchased by Winthrop Sargent of Massachusetts, who had been sent to the Natchez area to serve as the first territorial governor after the Spaniards evacuated in 1798. Gloucester was Sargent's home until his death in 1820.

AUBURN

Auburn is without question one of the finest buildings in the South. It was also designed by noted architect Levi Weeks who came to Natchez around 1808.[10] Some of his first commissions were to update existing houses by adding classic porticoes, i.e., Gloucester (1808) and Cherokee (1811).[11] He was also the architect for the Presbyterian Church, Bank of Mississippi, and the east wing of Jefferson Military College. The mansion named Auburn (1812) is probably his masterpiece.

In a letter dated September 27, 1812, Levi Weeks described Auburn to his friend Ep Hoyt in Deerfield, Massachusetts:

The brick house I am now building is just without the city line, and is designed for the most magnificent building in the territory. The body of this house is 60 by 45 feet with a portico of 31 feet projecting 12 feet supported by 4 Ionic collumns [sic] with the Corinthian entablature — the ceiling vaulted, the house two stories, with a geometrical staircase to ascend to the second story. This is the first house in the territory on which was ever attempted any of the orders of architecture. The site is one of those peculiar situations which combines all of the delight of romance — the pleasures of rurality and the approach of sublimity.

He further commented on Natchez and the owner of Auburn:

I am the more particular in describing this seat not only to give you an idea of the progress of improvement but to inform you what you will

Auburn — first classic style building in Mississippi (1812)

The rear of Auburn has been altered but the original lines can still be detected and appreciated. The rear doors are typical of the doors Levi Weeks used. (see Gloucester, Jefferson College). Two, two-story dependencies are located behind the house.

hear with pleasure — that the owner of it is a Yankey [sic] — a native of our own state Massachusetts and is now in Boston on a visit. His name — Lyman Harding — received his education at Cambridge, came to this country more penniless than myself — his celebrity as an attorney and counsellor at law has no competition in the territory — he has a little son (his only child) now in Boston. He has amassed a large fortune, owns an extensive sugar plantation in the Attakapas on the Bayou Teche. You will excuse this digression for I love to think and speak of my own countrymen who will not let the saucy Virginian and supercilious Carolinian ride them down.[12]

According to Edith Wyatt Moore, Harding died in 1820 and Mrs. Harding later married Daniel Vertner of Claiborne County. She went to preside over his home, Burlington. She must have leased Auburn to Dr. Stephen Duncan since the Trinity Episcopal Church history attributes the organization of the church to a discussion that was held among guests of Dr. Duncan at his home Auburn in 1821. When Lyman Harding's only son, Winthrop, reached age twenty-one in 1827, Auburn was sold to Dr. Duncan for twenty thousand dollars cash.

Auburn — door detail

A spiral stairway that architect Levi Weeks described as being geometric is in the Auburn foyer.

Auburn — architectural details

Dr. Duncan was a native of Carlyle, Pennsylvania, but had ties in Natchez since he was the nephew of the Postlethwaite brothers, who were among the earliest settlers of Natchez. While working as a physician in the Natchez area he met and married Margaret Ellis. She died at an early age leaving the doctor with two young children, who received a sizable inheritance including many acres of land. Eventually the doctor was devoting more time to managing plantations than practicing medicine. Around 1820 he married into another pioneer family when he claimed the granddaughter of Pierre Surget. Sometime after 1827 Dr. and Mrs. Duncan had the wings added to Auburn and equipped the house with elegant furnishings.[13]

Auburn mansion is probably better known by the local people than some of the other mansions because it now belongs to the public. The Duncan heirs deeded the mansion and surrounding acreage to the city of Natchez with the stipulation that it be used as a park. The park is one of the loveliest sections of Natchez, especially in the spring when the many dogwoods and massive azaleas are in bloom.

ARLINGTON

Arlington has everything a mansion is "supposed" to have: a handsome facade on a spacious building located in a parklike setting that combines natural beauty with planned formal gardens; dependencies to accommodate carriages, supplies, the kitchen, and servants' quarters; elegant furnishings (most are original with the house) set in enormous rooms — the hallway measures almost fifteen by fifty feet — with exquisite millwork and lofty sixteen-foot, eight-inch ceilings. The house contains such finishing details as marble window and door facings and a *fleur de lis* carved in wood blocks at each corner under the eave. Arlington was built in 1816 for Jane Surget White, the eldest daughter of Pierre Surget, one of Natchez' earliest families.

Arlington

ROSALIE

High on a Natchez bluff stands Rosalie, a red-brick mansion with tapered Tuscan columns. This house is important because of its site, its architecture, and personalities associated with it. The Rosalie tract was originally a part of old French Fort Rosalie established by Bienville in 1716 and named for the Countess of Pontchartrain, wife of the duc de Pontchartrain, the governor of Louisiana Territory. In 1729 the Natchez Indians massacred the residents of the fort. Following the signing of the Treaty of Paris, which gave Natchez to England, the

Rosalie

British repaired the fort and named it Panmure. When Baton Rouge was captured by the Spanish, the Spanish flag flew over Natchez and the fort. When the twenty-two acres became United States property (1798), the tract was offered for sale. After several owners, Peter Little purchased the property; he sold half of it in 1820 when he started building his mansion, which he named Rosalie. According to Natchez writer Edith Wyatt Moore, Rosalie does not occupy the exact site of the old fort but is situated near the portcullis.

Peter Little came to the Natchez area around 1800 and started the first sawmill in the region. Tradition has it that Mr. Little married his ward, Eliza Low, who was thirteen years of age, then sent her to school in Baltimore. Later, educated and matured, she returned to Natchez to a new, red-brick mansion with two-story Tuscan columns. The facade has fanlighted doors that open onto double galleries. Unlike most houses, only the central part of the facade is stuccoed.

The floor plan includes central hallways, double parlors that can be separated by sliding wooden doors, a library, a dining room, a re-

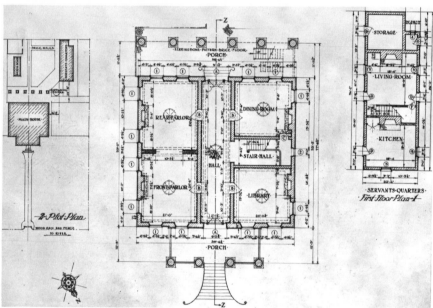

Rosalie — floor plan (HABS)

The Parsonage

cessed hall that contains a stairway which loops several times before reaching the attic; four bedrooms upstairs; a basement with storage rooms, wine cellar, and tool room. The basement floor is brick laid in a herringbone pattern (Photo: floor plan).

The beauty of the rear of Rosalie competes favorably with the facade (Photo). Six Tuscan columns rise two stories to support a hip roof. The first-floor gallery, like the basement, is paved with brick in a herringbone pattern. An outside stairway leads to the second-floor gallery that spans the width of the building. An arcade connects the two-story brick dependency containing the kitchen and servants' quarters to the main house. The design for Rosalie is attributed to James S. Griffen, brother-in-law of Peter Little.

Mr. Little must have been a very generous person since in 1850 he built a lovely, spacious house near his Rosalie to be used as a parsonage (Photo). Legend has it that his wife was a devout Methodist

Rosalie — fence containing no nails

Rosalie — rear view

Rosalie — rear view showing location of kitchen and walkway

who frequently entertained visiting ministers; therefore, to have some privacy in his own home, Little built and maintained a separate house for the ministers. The house is still referred to as "The Parsonage" even though trustees of the church sold it shortly after Little's death.

Rosalie was sold in 1856 to Mr. and Mrs. Andrew L. Wilson, who furnished the house with elegant mirrors, Belter parlor sets (twenty-two pieces), and Mallard bedroom pieces. Today the house is still furnished as it was by the Wilsons, since the house remained the property of the Wilson's adopted family until 1938, when it was sold to the Mississippi Society, Daughters of the American Revolution. The house is maintained as a shrine and is open to the public.

General Walter Gresham selected Rosalie to serve as headquarters for the Union forces in 1863. General and Mrs. U. S. Grant stayed at Rosalie while enroute from Vicksburg to New Orleans.

Rosalie, with its many trees, flowers, and shrubs is enclosed by a picket fence that is attractive, but not really exciting until closer examination reveals that the ancient fence is made of cypress and assembled without nails or pegs. The pickets fit into slots. There are three gates — one large gate for carriages and two small gates for pedestrians.

THE BRIARS

The Briars, like Gloucester, is important for its architectural elements as well as for the people who were associated with it. Located in a wooded setting high on a bluff near the Mississippi River, The Briars was the girlhood home of Varina Howell, second wife of Jefferson Davis, president of the Confederacy. The wedding (February 26, 1845) probably took place in the parlor, which is located to the right of the central hallway. This room contains a fine wooden mantel done in the style popularized by Robert Adam, the architect who designed during the Georgian period in England.

The story-and-a-half structure is more nearly a comfortable home in contrast to the elegant mansions that were constructed during this era. However, some of the details of the structure suggest that a trained architect was involved. The name of Massachusetts architect Levi Weeks is often associated with The Briars. The detail of the windows and doors is similar to that of buildings documented as being the work of Weeks (such as Auburn and Jefferson Military College).

The sloping roof of The Briars is broken by four dormers containing the interlacing arch pattern. The roof is supported by slender columns joined by a balustrade that stretches across the eighty-foot gallery. The house has many openings on all sides to catch any hint of a breeze in the days before air-conditioning. In addition to the four dormers, the facade is broken by six windows and three doors, with the central doorway containing double doors. Each of these doors is an object of beauty, with old glass forming a decorative pattern in the fanlight. The doors are enclosed in arched millwork.

The house is four rooms, plus a central hallway, in width. The hall has a vaulted ceiling with the arch repeated in the fanlight (Photo). The center hall leads to a recessed gallery that terminates with five attractive arches. Twin stairways rise from opposite sides of the gallery to give access to the four bedrooms upstairs. The central bedrooms were

The Briars — detail of arched ceiling and millwork

The Briars

divided by folding doors. When the doors were opened, a room of great dimensions was available for use as a ballroom, banquet hall, or for any affair requiring broad, open space.

The Rankin and Washington streets area of Natchez has many fine homes. Four of them — The Presbyterian Manse, Green Leaves, Elward, and Van Court — were selected to represent this area.

PRESBYTERIAN MANSE

A house with attractive fenestrations is the brick structure known as The Manse. The entry is emphasized by a large fanlight that spans the horizontally paneled doorway with sidelights and slender pilasters.

Presbyterian Manse

The extremities of the fanlight frame and the window lintels are decorated with pateras.

The Manse was built around 1820 and has been owned by the First Presbyterian Church since 1838. In the side yard is a study that was built in 1849.

GREEN LEAVES

Courthouse records indicate that as early as 1812 a fine dwelling house with appurtenances existed at this Rankin Street site. The prop-

Green Leaves

erty was purchased in 1849 by George W. Koontz who remodeled the house as a raised cottage with a classic portico. Doric columns support an entablature embellished with triglyphs. The doorway is emphasized by heavy millwork that frames side and transom lights of alternating circular and diamond panes. The cottage appearance is deceiving, however, because in addition to the four main rooms divided by a central hallway, the house also has side rooms with balconies outlined by iron, a rear bedroom wing and a two-story brick dependency that form a U-shaped courtyard. The courtyard is one of the loveliest in town with its ancient live oak tree providing shade for the spacious area.

Ownership of the home has remained in the George W. Koontz family since 1849. The house still contains its mid-nineteenth-century carpets, wallpaper, and furnishings.

ELWARD

In front of Green Leaves is Elward, a brick house with excellent proportions. The dominant feature of the house is the stepped gables. The house is fronted with an unpretentious portico that shields a simple doorway with side and transom lights.

Elward

VAN COURT TOWN HOUSE

The Van Court Town House is a lovely brick structure (now stuccoed) that was built by James Ferguson around 1835, approximately two years after his marriage to Josephine Quegles, daughter of Joseph Quegles who came to Natchez from Majorca, Spain. Already existing on the rear of the Washington Street lot was a two-story brick structure with galleries and an outside stairway. The two-and-one-half-story town house was built close to the street.

The town house is two rooms deep with side halls (Photo of floor plan). The plan has many similarities to 1830 town houses that were

Van Court Town House

constructed in New York at about the same time and are discussed in Talbot Hamlin's book *Greek Revival Architecture in America*. The low-pitched roof is broken by two delicate dormer windows that provide light for the garret bedroom. The asymmetrical door arrangement, emphasized by the ornamental ironwork, is the dominant feature of the facade. The slightly recessed door composition is especially captivating with slender sidelight separated from the door by pilasters, while the fanlight is separated by a simple entablature. The paneled door opens into a spacious twelve-foot by forty-two-foot hallway that contains a lovely stairway with a mahogany hand rail that loops to the third level.

To the left of the hall are the two main rooms on the principal floor — the parlor and the dining room. Sliding doors between these rooms are framed by Ionic pilasters in the parlor and millwork with square end blocks and a large central block on the dining room side. Both rooms have marble mantels, plaster ceiling medallions, and fine woodwork.

Ferguson's wife and three sons died between January, 1836, and May, 1837. Consequently he sold the house in 1838 to Dr. Andrew Macrery for twelve thousand dollars. In 1870 the property was sold to Adeline H. Baker, half-sister of Dr. Elias J. Van Court. This family occupied the house until 1899.

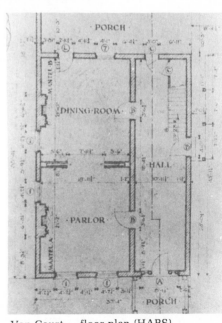

Van Court — floor plan (HABS)

The house was enlarged by adding a room to the left side of the house, and the exterior was covered with stucco sometime during the 1900s. The Van Court Town House is now the residence of Dr. and Mrs. Hall H. Ratcliffe, Jr.

WILLIAMSBURG

Williamsburg, a small, wood-frame, story-and-a-half structure, has probably occupied its site on Main Street since sometime before 1820. The lines of the slate roof are broken by a single central chimney and two attractive dormer windows that contain the interlacing arch pattern. A keystone marks the center of the dormer windows, while dentils outline the pediment. Similar dormers can be seen on Holly Hedges.

Eight chamfered colonettes support the gallery roof and are connected by a balustrade. The front wall has a dado, decorative millwork around the doors, and transom lights. The design in the transom is the radial pattern that was so popular in Natchez.

The original floor plan contained six rooms: two large rooms (nineteen feet square) and two small rooms downstairs, with two large bedrooms upstairs. A corner staircase with a cherry rail and newel posts rises

Williamsburg

Williamsburg

from the parlor on the left side of the house. The single center chimney has two fireplace openings downstairs and two upstairs. The downstairs mantels are done in the Robert Adam style, with the sunburst pattern.

The original detached brick kitchen is now gone. Williamsburg has been enlarged by having rooms added to the rear of the structure.

CHAMBER OF COMMERCE

The Natchez–Adams County Chamber of Commerce is to be commended for restoring as its headquarters a lovely house that was prob-

Chamber of Commerce

ably built around 1827 for J. C. Wilkins. The brick building has an exposed basement that is surrounded by a brick areaway. The stepped gables and the brick detail of the cornice are especially attractive.

Three elegant mansions with many classic features are D'Evereux, Melrose, and Dunleith. In general all three houses have simple exteriors with round, two-story columns with Doric capitals on D'Evereux and Melrose and Tuscan capitals on Dunleith. D'Evereux and Melrose have columns across the front and the rear, while Dunleith is surrounded by columns (peristyle). The central section of the Melrose facade is stuccoed, while all walls of D'Evereux and Dunleith are stuccoed and painted white. The buildings were probably painted white for at least two reasons. First, from a distance the buildings might look as if they were constructed of white marble, thus carrying further the Greek Revival theme. Originally the stucco on D'Evereux was marked to simulate marble slabs. Secondly, the white reflects sunlight, an important consideration in hot climates. The fenestrations on all three are simple and are arranged formally.

Since Greek temples did not have chimneys, the chimneys in Greek Revival houses were designed to be as inconspicuous as possible. This was done by having them inside the house and topped with very simple stacks. To soften the architectual severity of the buildings, decorative iron was used on the balcony at D'Evereux and on the galleries at Melrose and Dunleith. The Greek Revival detail inside is seen in the millwork and the acanthus-leaf medallions.

D'EVEREUX

D'Evereux, completed in 1840 for Mr. and Mrs. William St. John Elliot, plantation owners, has been featured in many books because of its outstanding architectural features and beautiful grounds. Its columns have capitals similar to those on the Parthenon with the Doric round echinus meeting a square abacus. The facade and roof line have a vague resemblance to the Mausoleum at Halicarnassus, with a cupola substituted for the statuary. The ceiling of the front gallery is enriched with three acanthus-leaf medallions, while the cornice combines

D'Evereux

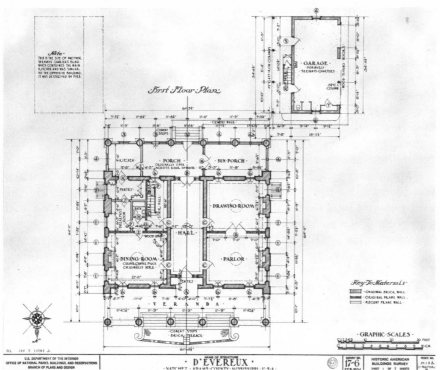

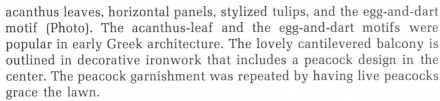

D'Evereux — floor plan

D'Evereux — porch detail

acanthus leaves, horizontal panels, stylized tulips, and the egg-and-dart motif (Photo). The acanthus-leaf and the egg-and-dart motifs were popular in early Greek architecture. The lovely cantilevered balcony is outlined in decorative ironwork that includes a peacock design in the center. The peacock garnishment was repeated by having live peacocks grace the lawn.

The recessed doorways are of the usual Greek Revival arrangement, with horizontal transoms spanning a paneled door with sidelights. The doorway ensemble is framed with Greek key millwork. A peculiarity of the gallery is the series of three flights of recessed steps.

Basically the rear of the house is the same as the front, but three features make it look very different. A second-floor gallery with a balustrade spans the entire width of the second level, while balustrades are also located between four sections of the lower level. This emphasizes the horizontal lines of the building and makes it look much wider. The horizontal line is emphasized still further by the wide, arched fanlights over the doors. This type doorway had been used most frequently in Natchez (instead of the horizontal transom) up to the present time. A terraced garden with shrubs and flowers placed informally leads from the rear of the house. The informal gardens, combined with the usually more restful horizontal emphasis, give the rear of the house an informal look, even though the elements are formally balanced.

The attractive, two-story building behind D'Evereux is now an apartment but was used in earlier years as a carriage house and servants' quarters. A building that matched this one and formed a U-shaped courtyard behind the main house was destroyed by fire. This building contained the kitchen, storage rooms, and servants' quarters. Another outside building that still exists is the privy, which was designed as a replica of the cupola. The designs for D'Evereux and the accompanying buildings are attributed to James Hardie. The floor plan shows the room arrangement. Note that the stairway is purely functional and is tucked

Melrose — double parlors

away in a small hall. This arrangement made the house much easier to heat.

The spacious grounds are lovely at all times but especially in the spring when thousands of tulips, iris, and azaleas are in bloom. It is easy to understand why a color photo of D'Evereux was selected to be used on the cover of the *Better Homes and Gardens'* publication *America's Gardens,* Time-Life book, *The Old South,* J. Wesley Cooper's *Antebellum Natchez,* and *The Majesty of Natchez* by Smith and Owen.

Only minor changes have been made in D'Evereux. A modern kitchen was installed in the butler's pantry following plans developed by the well-known Mutchler Brothers Company. The present owners, Mr. and Mrs. T. B. Buckles, Sr., and Mr. and Mrs. T. B. Buckles, Jr., are in the lumber business. To add their personal touch to the stately mansion, they had black walnut flooring installed over the original cypress floors. The floors were made by their lumber business from native southern black walnut trees.

Of particular historical note was a grand ball given in honor of Henry Clay when he visited the Elliots in December, 1843.

MELROSE

There have been no major structural changes in Melrose since it was constructed around 1845 by a lawyer named John T. McMurran. To emphasize this statement, Melrose still does not contain a kitchen. The outside kitchen in a nearby dependency has been maintained — but with modern appliances.

Ownership of Melrose has been with the same family since the property was sold in 1865 to Mr. George Malin Davis, also a lawyer, who was graduated from Yale. Each time the property has been inherited, there has been only one heir; therefore, the furnishings at Melrose have not been divided. Melrose passed from Mr. Davis to his only daughter, who married Dr. Stephen Kelly of New York, the son of a judge-banker. When Mrs. Kelly died at an early age, their only son inherited the property. For twenty-one years, Melrose was closed while the son was growing up in New York. Sometime after his marriage to Ethel Moore Kelly of New York (present owner) the couple visited Natchez. Mrs. Kelly did not know until she arrived in Natchez that Melrose was a furnished mansion. The furnishings are of museum quality with two of the settees being of rare designs.

Melrose, like Arlington, Auburn, D'Evereux, and many of the other mansions, is located in a park-like setting with a circular drive passing by a pond with picturesque cypress knees and numerous azaleas and native shrubs. The designer of Melrose is not known, but he introduced a new floor plan to the Natchez area when he used three rooms on the right side of the house (rather than two) that can be made into one long salon by opening the sliding doors. These three rooms were double parlors, plus a library. The doors between the parlors are framed with Ionic pilasters and spanned by a starburst pattern. Black marble mantels, paneled cornices, and acanthus-leaf medallions complete the architectural appointments (Photo: Door detail).

The length of the central hallway is broken by dividing it into a foyer section that runs parallel to the front parlor and a rear section that is the length of the two remaining rooms. The front foyer was lighted

Melrose

by diamond-shaped panes in the side lights and transom and by rows of candles over the doors.

To the left of the foyer is the dining room with a carved walnut punkah suspended over the dining table. When the punkah was used, a servant would pull a rope to keep it in motion to cool the diners and to keep insects away, since screens were not used at this early date. Behind the dining room is a long corridor that leads past a recessed hall and the butler's pantry to the detached kitchen. The recessed hall contains a lovely stairway that loops twice before reaching the upper levels.

The rear of Melrose is as picturesque as the facade with its two-story columns, galleries, and brick-paved walks that lead to some of the most interesting and attractive dependencies in the state (Photo). The building to the right had two kitchens on the lower level (one for the homeowner and one for the servants) with servants' quarters upstairs. Service buildings in Natchez were usually two stories high and only one room deep, with each room opening onto a gallery.

The second building located across from the first and at right angles to the main house contained work and storage rooms and an improvised

Melrose — rear view

cooling system for chilling food and dairy products. This room is usually referred to as the dairy. The room has waist-high, shallow cement containers, or troughs, to hold cool water. Hot milk or butter would be placed in the water to be chilled. Underneath these troughs was space for the vegetables to be placed on the cool brick floors. Beyond these buildings are the smokehouse and the privy.

Melrose is probably one of the best maintained antebellum structures in the South. The bricks are of fine quality and have aged well.

DUNLEITH

A private circular drive off Homochitto Street leads to one of the most imposing structures in the state. Dunleith is located on an elevated knoll which contributes to the "temple" appearance suggested by the two-story Tuscan columns that surround the house. Tuscan columns are an Italian variation of the Greek Doric order. The scroll-like brackets underneath the eaves and the style of the dormers are also Italianate.

The floor plan of Dunleith is similar to that of Rosalie and Arlington, with double parlors separated by sliding doors on the left side of the center hall; on the right the front room is separated from the dining

Dunleith

room by a recessed crosshall where a looping stairway rises to the upper levels. The floor length windows open onto the spacious galleries that are outlined with delicate iron grillwork. The architect for Dunleith is not known; however, Dunleith is very similar to Oak Alley, a house near Vacherie, Louisiana, that was designed by George Swainey.

The two-story rear dependency definitely has a Mediterranean look with its red bonnet-tile roof, stuccoed walls, small windows and doors with protective shutters, and long galleries that overlook a patio. This building contained the kitchen, storage rooms, and servants' quarters.

Dunleith was built for Charles G. Dalgreen after 1857. Today, the house is usually associated with the Carpenter family, since five generations of the J. N. Carpenter family have occupied Dunleith since 1886.

EDGEWOOD

Edgewood, like Mistletoe and Mount Repose, is located in the Pine Ridge Community on land that was granted to John Bisland by Spanish officials. The house was built in the early 1850s by Mr. and Mrs. Samuel Hopkins Lambdin (she was the daughter of William Bisland of Mount Repose and the granddaughter of John Bisland).[14]

The design of Edgewood indicates the beginning of a trend toward a more decorated look rather than the maintaining of the simple Classic style that had been in vogue in Natchez since about 1808 when Levi Weeks started adding Classic porticoes to existing houses. Notice that the capitals are Corinthian instead of the simple Doric or Tuscan. The facade also has some features that were promoted by the writings of Andrew Downing, such as the wide eaves supported by brackets and an arched window dominating the second floor. The arched window is emphasized by the broken roof line. Downing advocated decorating chimneys rather than concealing them because he considered a chimney to be a necessary part of the house. The panel chimneys on Edgewood show some decoration (compare with the simple chimneys of Rosalie and Dunleith).

The floor plan consists of eight rooms divided by central hallways. A handsome stairway dominates the rear of the hall.

Since the house was built on a hill, the rear of the house has three levels instead of two. The kitchen was located on the lower level, with a dumb waiter installed to lift the food to the main-floor dining room. A wing used for servants' quarters is located behind the house and

Dunleith — service ell has Mediterranean look

Edgewood

overlooks a paved courtyard. Two cisterns have been retained in this area.

The beauty of Edgewood is intensified by the lush green setting contrasting with the salmon-pink color of the stuccoed walls. The color of the house is still another feature that differs from the Classic era when houses were painted white and sometimes marked to looked like marble.

ELMS COURT

In 1852, Frank Surget bought one of the older two-story houses, with a Classic portico, as a wedding gift for his daughter Jane when she married Ayres P. Merrill, who was to be named by President U. S. Grant as the United States minister to Belgium in 1876. The Merrills enlarged

Elms Court

the house by adding the wings and changed the facade drastically by substituting decorative iron posts, arches, and balustrades for the heavy pillars. (Photo). The rear of the house received the same treatment, thus changing the formal Greek-temple appearance of the house to that of a villa.

Elms Court has a beautiful natural setting in a heavily wooded area. A circular drive leads to the spacious house that was a wedding gift for a second time about fifty years later, when James Surget gave Elms Court to his daughter Carlotta upon her marriage to David L. McKittrick. The present owner, Mrs. Douglas H. MacNeil, is the younger daughter of this couple.

STANTON HALL

In the 1850s an Irishman in Natchez named Frederick Stanton determined to build the most palatial mansion in a town known for its luxurious mansions. He accomplished this feat in a number of ways. First of all, the scale of his new home was much greater than its predecessors. The floor plan is three rooms deep divided by central hallways that run the length of the house. The two-story brick house with basement and cupola is located on a knoll, which makes it appear even larger.

The facade of Stanton Hall is much more decorated than those of other houses. Its fluted columns are capped with Corinthian capitals, dentils ornament the cornice, scrolls project from the pediment, Greek

Stanton Hall

motifs outline the coffered ceiling, ornate rose-patterned iron grillwork surrounds the galleries (the grill and floor curve around the columns on the upper level), and black and white marble squares pave the lower gallery. The recessed front door is emphasized by columns and pilasters with Corinthian capitals. Inside shutters can be used to cover the side-lights for privacy. The door is of two-and-one-half-inch-thick mahogany fitted with silver hinges and door knobs. Floor-length windows in the rooms on each side of the doorway ensemble can also be used for doors.

The design of the house (attributed to Thomas Rose) incorporates more architectual elements than other houses of the same decade, and

Stanton Hall — capitals correspond with plates in Minard Lafever's *The Beauties of Modern Architecture* (1835)

Stanton Hall—ornate door frame

each of these elements is very decorative. The parlor will be used to illustrate this point (Photo). The large room is visually divided into two rooms by triple arches that suspend from the ceiling. The ceilings in both sections are paneled and decorated with plaster medallions. A deep cornice incorporating Greek motifs outlines the top of the wall. Progressing from the ceiling downward, the next architectural features that demand attention are the decorative window and door frames. At first glance the side of the room that parallels the hallway may appear to be broken by numerous doorways. However mirrors are set in some of the decorative door frames. In addition, very large mirrors are used between the windows at each end of the right side of the house and over the mantels. Consequently, the very large room with elaborate bronze chandeliers and decorative architectural elements is reflected many times, thus making it appear even larger. The mantel in the parlor is of white marble and is probably the most decorated marble mantel in the state, with its carved designs of fruit, foliage, ribbons, and cupids (Photo).

Sliding wooden doors separate a music room from the parlor at the rear of the house. If an occasion demanded, the whole right side of the house could be opened into one grand salon with doors opening into the long hallway, a floor-length front window opening onto the elegant front gallery, and side windows opening onto a gallery trimmed with rose-patterned iron.

A library, a recessed hall containing a stair that loops several times before reaching the cupola, and a spacious dining room (forty feet by twenty-two feet) are located on the left side of the house. The library and dining room have marble mantels, ceiling medallions, and bronze chandeliers. Because of the length of the dining room, it has two mantels, two chandeliers, and two medallions. The bronze chandeliers in these rooms are very interesting because of the motifs employed. Indians, the first occupants of the Natchez area and for whom the town is named, are represented on the dining room chandeliers while the Frenchmen, who settled Natchez in 1716, are represented on the library chandelier.

The second level in most mansions was usually rather simple. At Stanton Hall the upper level is much simpler than the lower level but would be considered very decorative if compared to other mansions. For example, the six bedrooms have ceiling medallions, black marble mantels, and paneled millwork.

Ancient live oak trees and massive azaleas enhance the beauty of the mansion. The house and setting are enclosed by an exquisite iron fence with elaborate gates. The house is beautifully maintained by the Pilgrimage Garden Club, owners of the property since 1940.

Stanton Hall — elaborately carved white marble mantel in parlor

Stanton Hall — interior, double parlors. The ceiling design, the cornices and door trim correspond with plates in Minard Lafever's design books.

LONGWOOD

When Frederick Stanton finished his elaborate Stanton Hall, the Greek Revival style had reached its culmination in Natchez. This may have been one of several reasons why Dr. Haller Nutt went to an entirely different form and style when he selected a plan for his mansion in 1859. During the 1850s the octagonal form for houses was promoted by phrenologist Orson S. Fowler. Architects and carpenters in different parts of the United States experimented with the form. The octagonal shape had been used for centuries in Europe for churches,

Longwood

baptistries, and towers. Fowler advanced the theory in design books and magazine articles that the octagon was the ideal shape for domestic residences (read Mon Amour in Horn Lake section for further information concerning Fowler). In 1958 Carl Schmidt studied the octagon fad in the United States and found two hundred and sixty houses in twenty-eight states. Most of the houses were built in the 1850s with New York state having the most. Schmidt declared Haller Nutt's Longwood to be the largest and most beautiful octagonal house in the United States.[15]

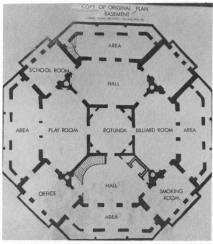

Longwood — floor plan

The plan for Longwood was based on an octagonal design prepared by Samuel Sloan, an architect from Philadelphia, who published a design entitled "An Oriental Villa, Design Forty-Ninth" in his 1852 Volume II edition of *The Model Architect.* Nutt engaged Sloan to adapt the design to his specifications. The revised plan was published in *Sloan's Homestead Architecture* in 1861 with this introduction:

> We enter upon our series by the presentation of a design adapted to the wants of the man of fortune in any section, but particularly suited for the home of the retired Southern planter. Aside from the novelty of the plan, it has every recommendation for convenience and utility that can be devised for a residence, where not only comfort but luxury is destined to reign. The occupants of such a residence are not only supposed to be wealthy, but fashionable people, and to possess in common with all the real aristocracy of every section, a character of hospitality, exhibited in the frequent entertainment of numerous guests, a liberal allowance of time and money for the purposes of social and convivial enjoyment. . . . A residence after this design is now being erected for a gentlemen in the vicinity of Natchez, Mississippi.[16]

The Haller Nutt family certainly qualified to live in the house described by the architect. Dr. Nutt, a scientist, inventor, landowner, and planter, was the son of Dr. Rush Nutt, who is mentioned in history books because of his improvements in the cottonseed variety, the Whitney cotton gin, and the cotton compress. Dr. Haller Nutt's mother was the daughter of Judge David Ker, first Territorial judge of Mississippi. Dr. Haller Nutt married Miss Julia Augusta Williams. The couple had eight children. By the 1850s, Haller Nutt had amassed a great fortune and was ready to build a mansion for his family. He broke from the Greek Revival style that had predominated in Natchez for almost fifty years and chose a thirty-two-room octagonal plan that the architect referred to as oriental because of its bulbiform dome and Moorish arches used in the woodwork. Due to the unusual design and elaborate plans for the house, Longwood has frequently been called Nutt's Folly.

The octagonal building (see floor plan) features a rotunda that is open for five levels — principal floor, second floor, third-story attic, observatory, and dome. The rotunda arrangement provided easy access to the adjacent rooms in addition to providing light and ventilation.

All of the rooms except the rotunda open onto either a balcony embellished with Moorish arches, reminiscent of those used on the magnificent Alhambra in Granada, Spain, or a veranda decorated with foliated drapery that was made in Philadelphia and shipped to Natchez via the *Ville France* on August 27, 1860.[17]

The wide arched windows that open onto the verandas might be referred to today as picture windows (Photo). These windows were

Longwood — picture window

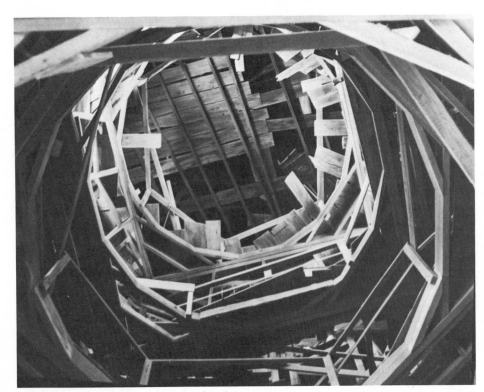

Longwood — rotunda construction detail

Longwood — stairway detail

designed to have sliding shutters that could be concealed in the five-inch hollow of the wall "a plan adopted to avoid the disagreeable appearance presented by a circular headed blind when open."[18] Many opportunities were provided for cross ventilation by the sixteen windows in the rotunda observatory, the triple windows opening onto the balconies, and the wide openings onto the galleries.

Heating the thirty-two-room mansion presented another problem. Four circular shafts, each measuring two and one-half feet in diameter were installed in the triangular areas where the rectangular rooms joined the octagonal rooms (see floor plan). Dampers were to be installed in the throat of each flue.[19]

According to architect Sloan's plans, the rooms were to be used as follows:

Longwood — brick detail

First, or principal, floor: Ceiling height 14 feet.
  Rotunda, octagonal in shape, diameter about 24 feet, tile floor. Main entrance hall with principal staircase, 20 feet by 34 feet. Marble floor. Drawing room, 20 feet by 34 feet. Reception room, 18 feet by 24 feet. Family room, 18 feet by 24 feet. Family room, 20 feet by 34 feet. Family room, 18 feet by 24 feet. Breakfast room, 18 feet by 24 feet. Dining room, 20 feet by 34 feet. Dressing rooms. Side and rear verandas.

Basement, or ground floor: Ceiling height 9 feet.
  Rotunda, octagonal in shape with closets in the angles. Lighted by strong glass in the floor over it and by lights in upper sections of the communicating doors. Billiard room. Staircase hall. Smoking room. Office. Playroom. Servants' hall. Sewing room. Store room. Areas beneath verandas.

Second floor: Ceiling height 12 feet.
  Staircase hall. Communicating gallery in the rotunda. Six chambers or bedrooms. Four verandas. Two wardrobes. Bathroom. A flight of stairs on the rear veranda extends from the basement floor to this one; another flight goes from the second floor to the attic floor.

Attic floor: Ceiling height 9 feet.
  Trunk room, 20 feet, 9 inches by 34 feet, with no fireplace. Three chambers, or bedrooms, each 20 feet, 9 inches by 34 feet. Each has a fireplace. Rotunda with a gallery.

These elaborate plans for the house were never executed. The initial construction began in 1860 and progressed at a rather rapid pace under the supervision of Philadelphians who were sent to the site to superintend the construction of what some people consider Sloan's masterpiece. Bricklayers and other specialists, as well as precut materials, were imported from Philadelphia. By the fall of 1861 the exterior was completed, with the exception of the exterior stairs and the installation of some of the windows and doors. By this time, however, the War Between the States had commenced. The Philadelphians laid down their equipment and fled to the North. Dr. Nutt managed to get the basement level completed (walls were plastered, floors finished, marble mantels installed). He moved his family into this segment of his dream home.

In 1864, Haller Nutt died, but members of his family occupied the basement of the unfinished mansion until 1968, when the heirs sold it

Longwood privy

to Mr. and Mrs. Kelley McAdams of Austin, Texas. In January, 1970, the McAdams family donated the unusual house to the Pilgrimage Garden Club. The house remains almost as it did in 1861, when the northern workmen dropped their tools and returned to Philadelphia. The unfinished state of the house makes it especially interesting to anyone concerned with construction techniques and materials (Photo: Rotunda detail, stairway and shaped corner brick).

Since Longwood is the largest octagonal house in the United States and one of the few examples of the oriental style, and in addition, was designed by a noted Philadelphia architect — Samuel Sloan — for one of the wealthiest men in the United States — Haller Nutt — the unfinished mansion has been designated as a National Historic Landmark. The house, which is open to the public, is unique in America and has been featured in many architectural publications.

KINGSTON METHODIST CHURCH

A small church near Natchez is included in the list of Historic American Buildings. The Kingston Methodist Church is a Greek Revival building constructed of brick, then stuccoed and marked to look like stone. The portico follows the Doric order.

Kingston Methodist Church

Washington

The small town of Washington (approximately eight miles east of Natchez) is one of the most historic towns in the state, having served as the capital city for the Mississippi Territory from 1802 to 1817. One of the first acts of the territorial legislature was to provide for the establishment of a college in Washington to be named in honor of the president of the United States, Thomas Jefferson.

JEFFERSON COLLEGE

The construction of a new building for Jefferson College did not come about until 1817, when a contract was let for the east wing. A letter dated May 24, 1817, from Levi Weeks to the trustees of Jefferson

Jefferson College

Jefferson College — president's home

College, indicates that he was the architect for the building. The second building was constructed to match the original building in 1838, while the central portion was added much later.

Jefferson Davis attended classes at the college, as did Albert G. Brown (who became governor of Mississippi), J. F. H. Claiborne, and B. L. C. Wailes, both noted historians. Among the faculty were John James Audubon, famous artist, and Joseph Holt Ingraham, author. Other names associated with the college are General Andrew Jackson, who camped with his troops on the grounds after his successful battle in New Orleans in 1815, and Aaron Burr, a former vice-president of the United States under Thomas Jefferson, whose preliminary hearings for treason in 1807 were held on the campus under the big oaks.

The college is being restored by the Mississippi Department of Archives and History and the Jefferson Military Academy Historical Committee for use as a state museum.

To the right of the entrance to the college is the house that was built for the college president (Photo).

INGLESIDE

Ingleside, a handsome house with fine Greek Revival millwork, became the home of Thomas Affleck, a noted scientist-writer who established an extensive nursery at Washington.

The center hallway of Ingleside can be divided by sliding wooden doors that are framed by pilasters. The parlor contains a marble mantel and decorative plaster work on the ceiling. An oddity in the house is the punkah carved in the shape of a lady. For the last century the house has belonged to the Rawlings family.

Ingleside

BRANDON HALL

The finest house in Washington is also one of the largest houses in Mississippi, with a central hallway that measures sixty-two by eighteen feet. The house was built by Gerard Brandon III, son of Mississippi's first native governor. The galleries that surround the wood frame house are especially attractive, with Ionic capitals on the lower levels and Corinthian on the upper. The galleries are enclosed with delicate iron grillwork (Photos). Jib doors open onto the galleries.

The house has a recessed front door, with sidelights and transom lights framed by Ionic columns and pilasters. The interior of Brandon Hall contains fine plasterwork and a curving staircase that rises from the rear of the central hall. The floor plan consists of six rooms, plus a central hallway, on each floor. The dining room has a punkah.

Brandon Hall

Brandon Hall — detail of iron work, second floor

Brandon Hall — detail of iron work, first floor

Wilkinson County

In Wilkinson County, south of Natchez, is Fort Adams, a ghost town today but a bustling port and fort city of yesteryear. Fort Adams was the American port of entry at the time that New Orleans was still under Spanish control.

In this vicinity were at least five houses of interest architecturally. Two of the houses, Curry and Murry, have been torn down; but the Cold Spring House, Salisbury House, and John Wall House still exist, though today they are in rather isolated areas and two of them are in dilapidated condition.

COLD SPRING

A pleasant surprise in a beautiful natural setting with massive azaleas and live oak trees is Cold Spring, with its four Tuscan columns supporting a steeply slanted roof. The house has double galleries outlined with iron rails, and the front door is framed with side and patterned transom lights.

Some unusual features of the house include a wine cellar under the stairway, a second-floor ballroom that extends the width of the house

Cold Springs

(folding doors can be used to divide the space), and a small bedroom with a corner fireplace that adjoins the ballroom.

The back of the house has been altered by enclosing the open archway. The iron gates with brass finials were originally a part of the arched opening ensemble (Photo). Cold Spring has been the home of the Reed family for four generations.

SALISBURY HOUSE

The Salisbury House struggles to survive near the community known as Pond. The beauty of the once substantial building can still be appreciated, even though the house must be classified as dilapidated.

A broad, sloping roof, broken by a single dormer, is supported by six stuccoed columns. The attractive doorway features arched millwork

Cold Springs — iron gate with brass finials was used across rear of house before the area under the arch was enclosed

Salisbury — gallery is behind the columns

Anglo American Art Museum at Louisiana State University

Salisbury—Federal style millwork

and a fanlight filled with interlacing arched panes. Two unusual features seen in the facade are the gallery located *behind* the columns (Photo) and bow windows in the room to the right.

Salisbury was constructed early in the ninteenth century by Moses Hooke of Maine who was a captain in Wilkinson's army. Hooke and his wife, Harriet Butler, originally from Carlisle, Pennsylvania, were among the first settlers of Wilkinson County.[20] Their house contained fine millwork part of which is now located in the drawing room, Federal Period, of the Anglo American Art Museum at Louisiana State University (Photo). The mantel and overmantel were executed in the style associated with Robert Adam, English architect.

The house is sometimes referred to as the Shepherd House. In 1829 Margaret Ann Hooke married C. M. Shepherd who was originally from Shepherdstown, Virginia, but came to Louisiana at the age of seventeen. The fine old structure needs attention soon if it is to be saved.

JOHN WALL HOUSE

To the casual observer the John Wall House might appear to be just another old house in a rural area. Upon closer examination, however, several fine features will be noted in the wood-pegged structure that dates to the late 1790s. The photo shows that the pegs are numbered.

John Wall House — recessed rear

John Wall House — wooden pegs were numbered

John Wall House

John Wall House — built during Spanish era

The first level is of brick with brick floors, while the upper, and main, level is of wood. Slender posts support the double galleries. The recessed front door is paneled and the edge of the door frame is ornamented with an intricate pattern (Photo). A transom is over the door. Formerly two flights of stairs led to the center of the second-floor gallery. The main entry was through double doors into a hallway. The second level has fine wooden mantels and a chair rail. The double-hung windows have small panes, twelve-over-twelve.

The back of the house has a recessed opening that shields the outside stairway. The decorative arched millwork is similar to the arch on the rear of Cold Spring. Remnants of formal gardens can still be seen on the front lawn. John Wall, a South Carolinian, was the alcalde (mayor or judge) for what is now Wilkinson County during the Spanish period.

ROSEMONT

The boyhood home of Jefferson Davis, who became president of the Confederacy, is near Woodville, the Wilkinson County seat. The house was completed in 1814 by Samuel Davis, who came to the area with his family from Kentucky. The simple wood structure with a gallery that spans the front of the house was occupied by members of the Davis family until 1896. The house remains as an excellent example of early southern architecture since it has never undergone any structural changes and has no modern conveniences. The interior has been repainted several times, but the original colors are being restored by Mr. Percival Beacroft, new owner of Rosemont. Mr. Beacroft, a Freeport, Texas, attorney, is being assisted in the restoration project by Mr. Ernesto Caldeira of New York. They were recently delighted upon finding letters from Jefferson Davis in a rat's nest within a wall. One letter was from Davis to his sister, written January 8, 1865.

In addition to the preservation of the house and the family cemetery, the rose gardens will be replanted, the detached kitchen and plantation outbuildings will be reconstructed, and an attempt will be made to recreate the atmosphere of a working plantation. Rosemont is open to the public.

Percival Beacroft

Rosemont — 1904

Rosemont — present day

LEWIS HOME

A wide brick walk leads to a stately red brick house with fanlighted doors. Known as the Lewis Home, this house was built for Dr. Thomas Lynn in 1832 and was purchased by Colonel John S. Lewis of Kentucky in 1836. The floor plan is typical of early southern Mississippi and Louisiana houses since it is one room deep with front and back galleries. A stairway rises from the back gallery (which has now been enclosed) to the second level, where folding doors can be opened to make the upper floor one grand ballroom.

Lewis Home

Port Gibson
and Claiborne County

In 1811 an area north of Natchez known as Port Gibson was incorporated. Fertile farmlands surrounded the town that was accessible from the Natchez Trace, Mississippi River, and Bayou Pierre. Planter's Hotel, located on Main Street, was built in 1817 to accommodate travelers. Today it is an apartment house (Photo).

Planter's Hotel

ENGLESING HOUSE

One of the oldest structures in Port Gibson is the Englesing House (1817), which has been occupied by Mr. Frank Englesing's family since 1850. The house is furnished with heirlooms of museum quality. Because the spacious cottage is a story and a half in the front and one story in the rear, it has a salt-box roof. A three-room ell is attached to

Englesing House

the rear of the house. A dominant feature of the Englesing House is the substantial end chimneys. Formal gardens that were laid out during the antebellum period and carefully maintained through the years are to the right of the house.

IDLEWILD

Idlewild was erected in the early 1830s by a Mr. Stamps who presented the raised cottage to his foster daughter when she married Mr. Louis Stowers of Port Gibson. The house has a hip roof, small dentils on the cornice, and doors that measure twelve feet in height. The fenestrations appear even taller since the windows and sidelights are floor length and the design of the millwork leads the eye upward. The door knobs are silver but the hinges are brass.

Idlewild

DISHAROON HOUSE

The largest antebellum house in Port Gibson is the Disharoon House, built by a planter named Cotten. Originally, spacious double galleries spanned both the front and rear of the house. Entry is through two heavily paneled doors that utilize the cross design. Triangular mullions and millwork with corner blocks further accent the entry. The center

Disharoon House

Disharoon House — spiral stairway

Disharoon House — hallway interior

Disharoon House — chandelier from Robert E. Lee steamboat

hallway ceiling is paneled and features a Della Robbia type plaster medallion (Photo). At the rear of the hall is a fine spiral stair (Photo).

Double parlors that can be separated by sliding wooden doors are to the right of the entry. The rooms contain black marble mantels and chandeliers that came from the dining room of the *Robert E. Lee* steamboat when it was dismantled (Photo).

The wooden structure on the front lawn is an example of home-crafted, dual-purpose playground equipment. In its present position it is a type of trampoline. It can be converted to a see-saw.

GAGE HOUSE

The Gage House was built by South Carolinian James A. Gage, who came to the Port Gibson area in 1827. The doorway of the house is especially attractive with the double doors heavily paneled in a horizontal pattern that becomes larger with each block in descending order. The transom lights are separated from the door and side lights by stepped millwork. The lower side lights can be raised for ventilation, another unusual feature (Photo).

The original floor plan consisted of four rooms — two down and two up — divided by central hallways. The bedrooms have doors that open onto the second-floor gallery. The attractive detached kitchen and service quarters still exist.

Gage House — kitchen and service quarters

Gage House — door detail

Gage House

Other historic structures in Port Gibson include the Port Gibson Bank, St. Joseph's Catholic Church, and the First Presbyterian Church. The bank was erected in 1840 as a hotel but has been used as a bank since 1890. The substantial brick building is fronted with six simple columns.

ST. JOSEPH'S CATHOLIC CHURCH

St. Joseph's Catholic Church (1850) is Gothic, with pointed arches and buttresses. The color blue predominates in the chapel as the natural light is filtered through blue window panes. The communion rail is intricately carved.

FIRST PRESBYTERIAN CHURCH

Probably one of the most photographed churches in Mississippi is Port Gibson's First Presbyterian Church (1859). The spire, topped by a twelve-foot hand with the index finger pointing heavenward is

Port Gibson Bank

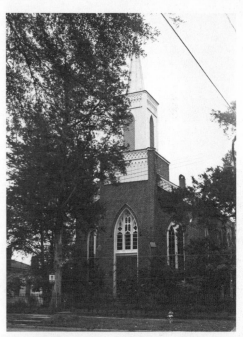

St. Joseph's Catholic Church

St. Joseph's Catholic Church — altar rail

First Presbyterian Church

unique. The original hand was of wood, carved by Daniel Foley. The ravages of time, aided by woodpeckers, caused the wooden hand to be replaced by a metal one in the 1890s. The church contains a gallery and has been lighted since 1880 by chandeliers from the old steamboat *Robert E. Lee.*

Southwest of Port Gibson are some interesting ruins and churches; namely, Windsor, the remains of a house that burned in 1890; Bethel Presbyterian Church; Oakland Chapel; and Rodney Presbyterian and Catholic churches.

WINDSOR

One of the most elegant mansions in the state was destroyed by fire in 1890. Random sections of a decorative iron balustrade connecting twenty-two towering Corinthian columns on paneled, stuccoed stiles are all that remain to remind present-day visitors of yesterday's splendor. One of the four flights of decorative iron steps that led to the main floor of Windsor can be seen in front of the chapel on the Alcorn A. &. M. campus (see photos of chapel).

The house was begun in 1859 for Smith Coffee Daniell II, a planter who was graduated from the local Oakland College and the University of Virginia Law School. According to a descendant, the house plan

Windsor

probably consisted of an exposed basement, a main floor, and a second floor with each level containing six rooms and a central hallway. A service ell extended from the rear of the house while a cupola crowned the roof.

The stark scene of the columns was used as the setting for part of the movie *Raintree County,* in which Montgomery Clift and Elizabeth Taylor starred.

BETHEL PRESBYTERIAN CHURCH

South of Windsor is the gemlike Bethel Presbyterian Church, founded in 1826 under the supervision of Dr. Jeremiah Chamberlain. Dr. Chamberlain, who came to Mississippi from Pennsylvania, was also responsible for starting Oakland College. General Grant landed his troops near here enroute to Vicksburg.

OAKLAND CHAPEL

Oakland Chapel was one of the first buildings constructed for Oakland College in 1830. The school, sponsored by the Presbytery of Mississippi with the Reverend Jeremiah Chamberlain as its first

Bethel Presbyterian Church

Oakland Chapel

Oakland Chapel — detail of iron steps

president, was one of the stronger antebellum colleges. The state of Mississippi purchased the college in 1871 for Alcorn University, later named Alcorn A. & M. The chapel, restored in 1959, is a three-story building fronted with six large columns. The iron steps that lead to the main floor are reported to have come from the Windsor mansion (Photo: Detail of steps).

The ghost town of Rodney has two interesting church structures. The **PRESBYTERIAN CHURCH** (ca. 1830) is a state shrine that belongs to the Daughters of the Confederacy. It is being restored under the auspices of the Rodney Foundation. The substantial red brick structure with fenestrations accented by rounded arches, has a stepped gable that leads to the octagonal bell tower. A reminder of the War Between the States is the cannonball that is lodged near the center area.

Rodney Presbyterian Church

Sacred Heart Catholic Church

SACRED HEART CATHOLIC CHURCH is the other church building of historic interest. Boards now hide the lovely windows of the Rodney Catholic Church (1868).

Vicksburg

Vicksburg is the destination each year for many tourists who journey to the port city to see the beautifully maintained 1,330-acre Military Park that is marked with over one thousand historic tablets, markers, monuments, and memorials; to go aboard the large sternwheeler, *The Sprague,* permanently docked on the Mississippi River; and to visit the Old Courthouse Museum, which is outstanding from the standpoint of both historic architecture and museum contents. In addition to these attractions Vicksburg has numerous historic homes.

OLD COURTHOUSE

The most imposing structure in Vicksburg is the Old Courthouse, located high on a terraced hill. Construction began in 1858 according to designs developed by the Weldon brothers — William, George, and Thomas. The building has a portico on each of the four sides. The east and west porticoes are fronted by six fluted columns with Ionic capitals; the north and south sides have four columns. The building is constructed of brick but has been stuccoed and scored to look like stone. Decorative iron is used for the balconies and to enclose a walkway around the octagonal tower.

Old Courthouse

The Old Courthouse is maintained today as a museum with emphasis on the antebellum and Civil War periods. The building is listed on the Registry of National Historic Landmarks.

SEARGENT S. PRENTISS BUILDING

Facing the courthouse is one of the oldest buildings in Vicksburg, the Seargent S. Prentiss Building, which is presently used as an office building for an architectural firm. When the building was being renovated, the architects found that the lower level of the building was of solid brick construction with brick floors, but the upper level of the building was half-timbered with brick fill, with timbers varying from ten by twelve to four by six.

The original floor plan probably contained four rooms—two downstairs (ceiling height of eight feet) and two upstairs (ceiling height twelve feet) with an outside stairway. The floors on the second floor are of eight- and nine-inch-wide cypress boards that are one and one-half inches thick. The mantels are also of cypress. The building was devoid of ornamentation except for a colonial beaded trim that has now been replaced. The stepped gables and the arched door add interest to the building.

Seargent Prentiss, frequently referred to in history books as the "silver-tongued orator" because of his way with words, moved his law office from Natchez to Vicksburg when the town of Vicksburg began to develop.

Seargent S. Prentiss Building

GOVERNOR McNUTT'S HOUSE

Governor Alexander McNutt built his house close to the street even though he had a spacious lot. The house has a simple facade with formal symmetry. These features reflect a similarity to houses in Virginia, the state from which McNutt migrated. In addition to developing a law practice in Vicksburg around 1824, he became a landowner, planter, and a state senator from Warren County. In 1837 he was elected governor of the state of Mississippi and was reelected in 1839 His home is being preserved by the Mississippi Historic Foundation of Vicksburg.

PLANTER'S HALL

Planter's Hall was probably one of the first buildings in Vicksburg to have architectural orders. Built as the headquarters for the Planter's Bank (on the first level) and a residence for Mr. Kuykendahl, bank president (on the second floor), the building has two lovely recessed doors. Corinthian capitals were used on the first level, while Doric capitals adorn the second level. The doorways differ in other details also, with the lower doorway having wood scored to look like masonry in the recessed area, slender side lights, and dentils that emphasize the line of the pediment; the upper level has a horizontally paneled door, interlacing arched panes in the transom, and a keystone that marks the center of the frame. The window lentils are decorated with a circular pattern on each corner, while a star-shaped motif ornaments the soffit. A bell-lyre patterned rail spans the facade.

When the bank ceased operation in 1842, the McRae family purchased the building to use as a residence. Members of this family occupied the

Governor McNutt's House

Planter's Hall

house until 1904, when the property was sold to the Canizaro family. In 1956 the Vicksburg Council of Garden Clubs purchased and restored the historic building for use as their headquarters.

PLAIN GABLES

Plain Gables, like the McNutt House, is a southern adaption of the New England colonial cottage achieved through increased ceiling and door height and enlarged windows. Built about 1830, its simple lines are devoid of ornamentation — hence the name, Plain Gables. An unusual feature is the elimination of lapped weatherboarding on the facade. The lovely iron entrance gate of the McCulloch Childs home has been sketched by many artists.

Plain Gables

Duff Green Mansion

DUFF GREEN MANSION

The Duff Green Mansion has sheltered many occupants since it was built initially as a spacious three-story mansion. The house has been a home, a hospital during the War Between the States, a home for elderly ladies, a home for orphan boys, and headquarters for the Salvation Army.

Decorative cast-iron is the predominant exterior feature. The interior of the house has been adapted slightly to meet the varying needs of its diversified occupants. The floor plan follows the Greek Revival pattern with a central hallway dividing four rooms on each level. A variation in the Duff Green house is a back hallway that contains the stairway. Double parlors are located to the right of the entry. These rooms can be divided by sliding doors. Floor-length windows open onto the gallery. The ceilings are decorated with medallions in the acanthus leaf and grape patterns. The mantels are white marble.

ANCHUCA

A Greek Revival mansion in the old section of Vicksburg is Anchuca. The dentils, the two-story columns, and the doorways with side and transom lights indicate the style. A brick dependency that contained the kitchen is located behind the house. The rear patio is paved with hundreds of bricks and is beautifully landscaped.

CEDAR GROVE

John Alexander Klein, a businessman-planter, built his stately brick mansion on a bluff overlooking the Mississippi River. The river traffic could be observed from the double galleries lined with elegant iron rails. The floor-length windows and Greek Revival doorways give easy

Anchuca

Cedar Grove

access to front and rear galleries. Four Tuscan columns front the principal and rear facades.

Entry is into the central hall that has a straight stairway rising along the left wall for approaching the bedrooms on the second level. To the right of the entry on the first floor are double parlors with sliding doors, marble mantels, plaster ceiling medallions, and exquisite gold cornices that span the floor-length windows and pier mirrors (Photo). A bedroom and the dining room are located on the left side.

As his family and fortune increased, so did Klein's house. Around 1852 the south side of the house was enlarged by three rooms: a library to the right of the front parlor, a spacious ballroom to the right of the back parlor, and a conservatory between the library and the ballroom. The ballroom was probably one of the finest in the state with its windows and three doors divided by pier mirrors that reflected the crystal chandeliers, the decorative plaster work, the marble mantel, and the Mississippians dressed in their finery for the balls. In 1858 the first level on the north side of the house was enlarged by adding a dressing room, a nursery, a hallway, and a new dining room. The original dining room was converted into a ladies' parlor and extended to include part of the back gallery. Between 1880 and 1882 a bay window with Italianate brackets was added to the nursery.

The rear of the house is like the front but the floor is flush with the ground where the wooden floor of the gallery meets a patterned brick walk. A flight of ornamental iron steps leads to the second-story gallery (Photo). The terraced grounds are landscaped informally and accented with urns and a delightful iron gazebo.

The house remained in the Klein family until 1919, when it and its

Cedar Grove — parlor

Cedar Grove — detail of mantel and cornice in the ballroom

Cedar Grove — rear view, iron steps

furnishings were sold to Antoine Tonner. The ownership changed again in 1936, when Dr. Augustus John Podesta bought the property. To save the mansion from destruction in 1960, the Vicksburg Theater Guild purchased it and maintains it today as a museum.

McRAVEN

Probably the most unusual house in Vicksburg is McRaven. Like many of the Natchez houses, McRaven "grew" through the years. The rear wing is the oldest section. It is two stories, one-room wide with a gallery. The front section of the house is a later addition that follows a town house plan. It includes architectural features that were popular during the Greek Revival period: a flying-wing stairway, marble mantels, jib doors, plasterwork, and heavy millwork. The long, narrow town house plan is rather surprising since the house is located on a spacious lot.

The house was occupied for ninety years by three sisters who were recluses. The house appeared unkept but structurally sound when Mr. and Mrs. O. E. Bradway, Jr., purchased it and many of its nineteenth century furnishings. The house has been beautifully restored and is open to the public.

McRaven

NOTES TO PART ONE

1. D. Clayton James, *Antebellum Natchez* (Baton Rouge: Louisiana State University Press, 1968), pp. 29, 240.

2. Jack D. L. Holmes, *Gayoso* (Baton Rouge: Louisiana State University Press, 1965), p. 125.

3. *Ibid.*, p. 120.

4. Harnett T. Kane, *Natchez on the Mississippi* (New York: Wm. Morrow & Company, 1947), p. 95.

5. Holmes, p. 121.

6. *Ibid.*, pp. 198, 199.

7. Kane, p. 110.

8. Personal interview with Bethany Lambdin, Natchez historian and mistress of Mistletoe.

9. James, pp. 29, 240.

10. Family papers presented to the Mississippi Department of Archives and History by Miss Katie D. McClutchie, great-great granddaughter of Levi Weeks.

11. James, p. 240.

12. Weeks to Hoyt, September 27, 1812, Levi Weeks and Family Papers, Mississippi Department of Archives and History.

13. Article by Edith Wyatt Moore in *The Natchez Times*, December 7, 1952.

14. Mary C. Cunningham, "The Development and Appreciation of Historic Architecture at Natchez, Mississippi," M.A. thesis, George Peabody College for Teachers, 1930, p. 73.

15. Carl Schmidt, *The Octagon Fad* (Scottsville, New York, 1958), p. 45-46.

16. Samuel Sloan, *Sloan's Homestead Architecture* (Philadelphia: J. B. Lippincott and Co., 1861), pp. 57, 60.

17. Bill for materials delivered on board ship *Ville France*, Aug. 27, 1860. Copy of bill obtained from Perkins Library, Duke University.

18. Sloan, p. 61.

19. *Ibid.*

20. *Biographical and Historical Memoirs of Mississippi* (Chicago: Goodspeed, 1891), Vol. II, p. 758.

PART TWO

Jackson

Canton

Sandy Hook

Jackson

Jackson, almost centrally located in the state, has been the capital city since 1822. It is not surprising, then, that three of the finest public buildings in Mississippi are in this city: the Old Capitol, the Governor's Mansion, and the New Capitol. We are fortunate still to have the Old Capitol and the Governor's Mansion, since many antebellum buildings in Jackson were destroyed by fire in 1863 under the direction of General William Sherman. For many years immediately following the fire, the city of Jackson was referred to as "Chimneyville." Other buildings that escaped the flames were the City Hall, The Oaks, and the Manship House.

OLD CAPITOL

The Old Capitol building was an ambitious project for a state that was only sixteen years old. Ninety-five thousand dollars were allocated for the statehouse, and building commenced under the direction of architect John Laurance of Nashville, Tennessee. In the initial stages of construction, a legislative committee determined the building to be "manifestly defective," and the architect was dismissed by Governor

Old Capitol

Old Capitol — porch detail

Old Capitol — dome detail

Old Capitol — ornate millwork

Hiram Runnels. In 1836, William Nichols, an English architect with offices in Philadelphia, was appointed state architect. Nichols had designed a state capitol for Alabama in Tuscaloosa in 1826, and soon afterwards he submitted plans for a group of buildings for the University of Alabama. His established reputation was greatly enhanced after the Mississippi capitol was completed. The handsome building has six finely executed Ionic columns that support a simple pediment. The ceiling of the portico is coffered, while elegant iron rails outline the main floor. Rosettes adorn the window lintels. The dome that covers the rotunda is approximately 120 feet high (Photo).

Entrance to the building is under brick arches into a vestibule that has twin spiral stairways. Beyond the entry hall is the spacious rotunda, with wings extending from two sides. The doorways along the long wings have decorative millwork, revealing patterns similar to those in Minard Lafever's design books. The building was completed in 1839 at the cost of $400,000.

The building is beautifully maintained today, though this has not always been the case. After about fifty years the capitol building was too small to accommodate the needs of a government for a growing state. Therefore, a new building was commissioned with Theodore C. Link, architect from St. Louis, in charge (Photo: New Capitol located at Mississippi and Congress streets). The seat of government was moved to this building in 1903, while the old building merely existed until someone decided, in 1916, that the space could be used to house state offices. To use the space efficiently the spiral stairways were removed

New Capitol

and the house and senate chambers were torn out. When the building was restored for use as a historic museum in 1959, these areas were reinstated according to the original design.

GOVERNOR'S MANSION

As state architect, William Nichols was also responsible for designing the Governor's Mansion. He reported to the legislature that he "intended to avoid a profusion of ornament, and to adhere to a plain republican simplicity, as best comporting with the dignity of the state."[1] To achieve this goal he planned a rectangular building seventy-two by fifty-three feet with a formal arrangement of fenestrations, separated

Governor's Mansion

vertically by pilasters. The severity of the boxlike design is relieved by an elegant semicircular portico enhanced with fine Greek Revival details, such as the coffered ceiling, dentils, and fluted columns with Corinthian capitals. The source for the design of the capitals appears to be Plate Number 43 in Minard Lafever's design book, *The Beauties of Modern Architecture,* published in 1835.

The monumental front door has side and transom lights of lead glass, which probably replaced regular rectangular panes when the building was modernized in 1908. The entrance into the mansion is spectacular and may require a few moments to absorb the details. The vestibule is octagonal in shape, with the octagon form repeated in the ceiling plaster design. The room has deep cornices comprised of classic motifs in plaster. The angled walls have niches for statuary. The entrance hall has freestanding and engaged columns with Corinthian capitals that framed an original curved stairway (removed during the 1908 modernization, but soon to be replaced according to the original design).

The decorative plasterwork and millwork in the house are especially fine (Photo). The design for the door detail is similar to Plate Number 25 in Lafever's 1835 publication. Plate Number 46 for chimney piers or mantels was also used. It is not known if the finishing details for the mansion were executed locally by artisans using the Lafever design book or if these architectural ornaments were made elsewhere and imported. It is important to note, however, that John Gallier (brother of James Gallier, famous New Orleans architect who was in partnership with Lafever in New York before coming south) was engaged in manufacturing architectural ornaments in New York during the period his brother was in partnership with Lafever.[2] Stanton Hall in Natchez has architectural details that are similar to these and of the same superb quality.

The original part of the mansion consists of: (1) a *basement* with eight-foot ceilings (According to architect Nichols the rooms were to

Governor's Mansion—Lafever style door detail

Governor's Mansion—plaster in foyer

Governor's Mansion — capital detail compares with a Minard Lafever plate

Governor's Mansion — cornices

be used as servant's rooms, storerooms, and a cellar.); (2) *principal* floor with a drawing room that measures fifty by twenty-four feet, a dining room with folding doors that can be combined with another room to measure the same length as the drawing room, and the octagonal entry, plus the staircase hall; comfortable family rooms in the rear of the building; (3) *second floor* with four spacious chambers, a wardrobe, and a private staircase that connects with the basement level.[3]

The fate of the elegant but out-of-date mansion was at stake early in the twentieth century. A decision had to be made either to invest money in the building to make it more livable for the state's chief executive or to sell it. Thirty-thousand dollars were appropriated in 1908 to renovate the old building for state occasions and to erect an annex for more contemporary family accommodations. The stairway was vastly changed at this point. In 1961 the building was restored. Only ten years later the building became the subject of debate again when the mansion was declared by building inspectors to be unsafe for habitation. Money has been appropriated to repair and restore the historic mansion and to update the annex.

JACKSON CITY HALL

Another stately public building is the Jackson City Hall, completed in 1847 at a cost of approximately $7,500. The original design of the

Jackson City Hall

building is attributed to William Gibbon. The City Hall was altered by enlarging the edifice in 1853 and by adding columns to the back of the building around 1928.

THE OAKS

The National Society of the Colonial Dames of America in the State of Mississippi bought the small cottage that was built by a former mayor of Jackson, James H. Boyd, to use as its headquarters. The house

The Oaks

consists of four rooms divided by a central hallway. A detached kitchen, cistern, and dairy house were located behind the house.

MANSHIP HOUSE

When Charles H. Manship planned a new house for his large family in 1857, he was influenced more by the writings of Andrew Jackson Downing than by the prevailing Greek Revival style. The front of the house, which faces Northwest Street, has many similarities to Figure 128 in Downing's book *The Architecture of Country Houses,* published in 1850. Manship House is smaller and has less detail than Downing's cottage-villa in the Rural Gothic style. But similarities exist in the projecting central part of the house that has a dramatic gable outlined with a decorative bargeboard, in the pointed-arch windows, in the pointed-arch opening onto the porch, in the double doors with pointed-arch millwork, and in the spacious side galleries with ornamental supports. Manship did not ignore the Greek Revival completely since dentils were used on the facade and the millwork on the inside is more Greek than Gothic.

The house also has a side porch which Downing promoted for comfort and irregularity of form. Floor-length windows open onto the front and side galleries. More people probably recognize the side porch of Manship House since it has been "the front" for many years (Photo). Some of the beautiful ironwork was taken from the original front of the house and added to the side gallery to give it more importance.

The attention of some people who drive by Manship House may be attracted more by the large bell on the lawn rather than the cottage now nestled under shrubs and trees that have been growing for decades. The bell belonged to the Volunteer Fire Department of which Mr. Manship was head because he was the mayor of Jackson. When Mr. Manship retired he was given the bell which was considered a rare gift since many bells were melted to make bullets for the war.

The detached kitchen has been attached and the chimneys sealed. Otherwise Manship House has been altered very little since 1857.

Manship House — original front porch detail

Manship House — original front. The design contains many features promoted by Andrew Jackson Downing.

Manship House — the side porch became the front. The large bell once belonged to the volunteer fire department of Jackson.

Hinds County Courthouse

Ownership of the house and many of the original furnishings remain within the family of the builder.

HINDS COUNTY COURTHOUSE

The Hinds County Courthouse in Raymond was designed by the Weldon brothers, George, William, and Tom, who also designed the Old Courthouse in Vicksburg. The Scotch-Irish immigrants were known as "gentleman builders" in the Port Gibson–Vicksburg area.

CHAPEL OF THE CROSS

A beautiful little chapel located in a wooded area north of Jackson in Madison County is significant because of its style and the socio-economic conditions that led to its establishment. The chapel was built by Mrs. Margaret L. Johnstone as a memorial to her husband, John T. Johnstone, who was a wealthy landowner-planter.

Construction of the chapel began in 1850. The design of the structure is very similar to the sketch of a "first-pointed" church by Frank Wills that appeared in the *New York Ecclesiologist,* II (October, 1849). The plan was adapted to meet the local situation, a plantation chapel, by omitting the tower and transepts. Both oral tradition in the Johnstone family and Phoebe Stanton in *The Gothic Revival and American Church Architecture; An Episode in Taste, 1840–1856,* attribute the design of the chapel to Frank Wills, an English architect who became the official architect for the New York Ecclesiological Society.[4] The Grace Episcopal Church in Canton (also in Madison County) is listed in the July, 1853, *New York Ecclesiologist* as a Frank Wills design.

The resident clergyman who held services in the Johnstone house and in a nearby schoolhouse while Chapel of the Cross was under construction was the Reverend John Freeman Young (1820–1885), who

Chapel of the Cross — note the asymmetrical placement of the door

Chapel of the Cross — designed by English architect Frank Wills

later obtained a doctor of divinity degree from Columbia College, became assistant minister at Trinity Church in New York, and eventually was named second Bishop of Florida.[5]

The Chapel is approached from the west side (Photo) where the "pointed look" is achieved by buttresses that go beyond the steeply pitched roof to form a bell cote and by pointed-arched windows. The entrance is placed asymmetrically on the south side (Photo) of the Chapel and is emphasized by the dramatic lines of the roof and the pointed-arch doorway closed by an iron gate and wooden doors. The pointed-arch motif is repeated on the interior in the woodwork and plaster labels.

The Chapel has had sporadic attention since its consecration in 1852. In 1956 the building became the restoration project of the Dancing Rabbit Creek Chapter of the Children of the American Revolution sponsored by the Magnolia State Chapter of the Daughters of the American Revolution. The National Society of the Children of the American Revolution was also involved in the restoration project. The major changes in the structure since 1852 include the windows, where colorless, opaque glass replaced the original stained glass, and the roof, where an asbestos covering replaced the cypress shingles. Some of the original furnishings are still used. Chapel of the Cross is one of the best examples of Gothic church architecture in the state.

Many family burial plots are enclosed by decorative iron fences in the cemetery behind and to the side of the Chapel of the Cross. The fence that surrounds the Johnstone family plot is a unique combination of leaves, flowers, and vines on gnarled branches (Photo).

Chapel of the Cross — unusual ironwork

ANNANDALE

After the Chapel was completed, Mrs. Margaret Johnstone had a three story Italianate villa built nearby for herself and her daughter. The plan for the house appeared in Minard Lafever's book *The Architectural Instructor* (1856) as Villa No. 4. The millwork was supplied by the Hinkle, Guild and Co. of Cincinnati, Ohio. Mr. J. Larmour of Canton supervised the construction.

The house was destroyed by fire.

Annandale—destroyed by fire. This elevation for the house appeared in a Minard Lafever publication.

Canton

Canton, located near the Big Black River, Pearl River, and the Natchez Trace, was incorporated in 1836. Developed around a town square, Canton's downtown area has been dominated since 1852 by a magnificent courthouse building (Photo). The Greek Revival building has Doric columns and a deep frieze ornamented with triglyphs. Constructed of brick, it has a low roof crowned by a cupola, and its grounds are enclosed and enhanced by an iron fence.

Madison County Courthouse

Grace Episcopal Church — designed by Frank Wills

Grace Episcopal Church — interior

GRACE EPISCOPAL CHURCH

Half a block east of the courthouse is a small Gothic church that was built shortly after the Chapel of the Cross at Mannsdale. The tower, arches, and pinnacles contribute to the pointed style that its designer, English architect Frank Wills, promoted in his writings as the official architect for the New York Ecclesiological Society. The Grace Episcopal Church is listed in the July, 1853, *New York Ecclesiologist* as a Frank Wills Design.

Two houses east of the courthouse that are especially noteworthy are the Shackleford House, still occupied by descendents of the builder, and the Mosby House.

SHACKLEFORD HOUSE

Shackleford House is a mid-nineteenth-century building constructed by Mr. C. C. Shackleford, a lawyer. The two-and-a-half-story brick building with a simple one-story portico is a good example of the Federal style. The house has remained in the family of the builder and contains some original furnishings.

Shackleford House

MOSBY HOUSE

In 1856 Colonel William Lyons built the large brick mansion that is known today as the Mosby House. The late date—1856—accounts for the amount of decoration on the basic Greek Revival structure. The brackets and the arched windows in the cupola are Italianate features. The Greek Revival lines predominate, however, with the two-story columns supporting a triangular pediment outlined with dentils. The doorway arrangement with side lights, transom lights, pilasters and dentils is also characteristic of Greek Revival buildings.

A curving stairway in the central hall leads to the upstairs apartments. A separate spiral stairway curves to the cupola level. According

Mosby House

to tradition, Colonel Lyons left for a tour of Europe while his mansion was being constructed. When he returned he soon learned that there was no approach to the observatory. To rectify this mistake, a spiral stairway was installed in the central hallway on the second level to give access to the third level.

Sandy Hook

JOHN FORD HOUSE

One of the best examples of pioneer houses is the John Ford House located near the Pearl River. This house has some features similar to the early Spanish houses in Natchez. The two-and-a-half-story structure is brick on the lower level and wood on the upper levels. The large beams are put together employing the mortise and tenon method of

Marion County Historical Society

John Ford House

John Ford House—pegged construction

construction and then anchored with wooden pegs (Photo.) The large Roman numerals that are cut into the beams suggest that the logs were cut to fit and then the matched sets were numbered for easy assembling. The many square nails help to identify the building as being an early structure.

John Ford's name has been associated with the building since the the early 1800s but the exact construction date of the house and the name of the builder are uncertain. John Ford, a South Carolinian, was described by J. F. H. Claiborne as ". . . a farmer and a man of fine sense and unimpeachable integrity — of patriarchal influence." He was a leader in the territorial area outside of Natchez. In 1816 the Pearl River Convention was held at his house. This meeting consisted of backwoods people who opposed the Natchez leaders' proposal for state boundary lines. A delegate was elected at the Pearl River Convention to represent the group in Washington. Boundary lines were agreed on and Mississippi became a state in 1817. Ford was a delegate from Marion County to the convention to form a constitution for the state of Mississippi.

The Ford House is also important because it was the site for the Second Mississippi Methodist Conference. According to legend, Ford was a devout Christian and reportedly asked Andrew Jackson to refrain from using profanity while in his house! Because the house was located near Jackson's Military Road and near the Pearl River, travellers often stopped at the Ford House. At one time a room in the house was used as a territorial post office. The Ford House certainly deserves to be called "historic."

NOTES TO PART TWO

1. Nichols' report to the Committee on Public Buildings, February 12, 1840.

2. Denys Peter Myers in the new introduction to Minard Lafever's *The Beauties of Modern Architecture* (1835) reprinted by Da Capo Press (1968), p. ix.

3. Nichols' report.

4. Phoebe Stanton, *The Gothic Revival and American Church Architecture* (Baltimore: John Hopkins Press, 1968), p. 293.

5. Dawn Mattox, Chapel of the Cross nomination form for the National Register of Historic Places, Mississippi State Department of Archives and History, February, 1972.

PART THREE

Biloxi

Ocean Springs

Gautier

Pascagoula

Biloxi

The Gulf Coast is known for its favorable climate and good fishing rather than for excellent farm land. Therefore, instead of stately mansions, there are more modest homes designed to take advantage of the coastal location. This area was first settled by Frenchmen, then Spaniards. Reminders of this early period are street names and several buildings.

FRENCH HOUSE

According to local historians, the French House may have been constructed as early as 1737 when Biloxi was settled by the French. The one-and-a-half-story painted brick structure has a front portico sup-

French House

ported by four pillars joined by a decorative iron grill. The facade features an asymmetrical entry with French doors. The fenestrations are emphasized by heavy wooden shutters that can be closed for protection. Iron bracing beams, used for construction stability, can be identified from the exterior by the S–shaped design near the attic.

The original floor plan consisted of four rooms on the main floor, a cellar, and one room upstairs that was accessible via an outside stairway.

SPANISH HOUSE

The stalwart, colonial structure on West Water Street is believed to have been constructed for a Spanish army captain who was sent to Biloxi as commanding officer when the West Florida Territory came under Spanish dominion. The house is constructed with brick walls of from twelve to fifteen inches in thickness. White sand was poured

Spanish House

Old Brick House

between the bricks for insulation. Oyster-shell cement plaster was used to stucco the exterior walls. The stepped roof was sheathed with cypress boards, then covered with slate. Details concerning the original balcony were revealed when a frame porch was removed in recent years. The balcony was thirty inches deep and extended the width of the building.

The original floor plan consisted of seven rooms. The ceiling height for the four rooms on the first floor is ten feet, and the second floor ceiling height is eight feet. The interior walls are plaster on brick with cypress used for mantels and doors. The floors are of random-width pine.

OLD BRICK HOUSE

The Old Brick House on East Bay View Avenue has been the restoration project for the city and garden clubs of Biloxi.

RALPH WOOD HOUSE

Mr. De'Buys from New Orleans had this raised cottage built for his daughter Dorsette Richars. The house has brick construction on the lower level and wood for the upper floor. The original steps at the front were probably like the board ones at the rear of the house,

Ralph Wood House — paneled ceiling

Ralph Wood House — rear view

Ralph Wood House

Gillis House

which are similar to those at Beauvoir. Note the outside stairway on the back gallery that leads to the upper floor (Photo). An unusual interior feature is the paneled ceiling in the central hallway (Photo).

GILLIS HOUSE

The Gillis House was damaged by Hurricane Camille in 1969 and will probably be demolished. The architectural style is interesting because of the recessed porches on three sides and the broad eaves — examples of how local weather conditions can influence building styles. The eaves helped to shade the house to keep it cool, while the porches provided a place to sit to enjoy the prevailing breezes. The porch on the west (left) side has an outside stairway that leads to the upper floor.

EPISCOPAL CHAPEL

Jefferson Davis, president of the Confederacy, attended services held in this small chapel. When the more imposing Church of the Redeemer was constructed in front of the chapel, the Jefferson Davis family pew

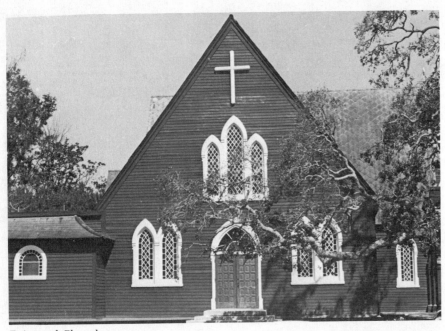

Episcopal Chapel

was moved to the new church. In 1969 Hurricane Camille destroyed the Church of the Redeemer, except for the bell tower. The chapel, which had been converted to the parish house, is now the church once again.

WOODLAWN

Although scarred by the destructive forces of Hurricane Camille, Woodlawn is still one of the most elegant structures in the South. The beauty of the mid-nineteenth century building is enhanced by the setting of live oak trees and a Gulf of Mexico frontage.

The original floor plan of Woodlawn was typical of those in southern Louisiana: one room deep, three rooms wide and two or three stories high. Each room on the first and second floors had windows and doors that opened onto the front and back galleries. The two main rooms on the principal floor had marble mantels and parquet floors. Before

Woodlawn

Camille, a decorative outside stairway could be seen rising from the right side of the lower portico, changing directions midway before ascending to the second level.

In the early 1900s, the back gallery was enclosed for use as a kitchen and dining room. The original kitchen and servant quarters are located in the rear yard and compliment the main house. The house was built for Mr. T. C. Toledano.

BEAUVOIR

Beauvoir is the most historic house on the Mississippi Gulf Coast, since it was the last home of Jefferson Davis, the only president of the Confederacy. The house and accompanying cottages are maintained today as southern shrines.

Beauvoir is a raised cottage which is much larger than it appears in photographs. The house was constructed in 1852 by James Brown, a planter from Madison County, Mississippi. Local weather conditions probably influenced Mr. Brown in designing the new house. For example, a raised cottage allowed breezes to flow under the house to cool the floors. Long spacious galleries helped to shade the house and

Beauvoir

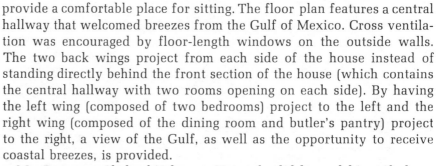

Beauvoir — door detail

Beauvoir — front parlor

provide a comfortable place for sitting. The floor plan features a central hallway that welcomed breezes from the Gulf of Mexico. Cross ventilation was encouraged by floor-length windows on the outside walls. The two back wings project from each side of the house instead of standing directly behind the front section of the house (which contains the central hallway with two rooms opening on each side). By having the left wing (composed of two bedrooms) project to the left and the right wing (composed of the dining room and butler's pantry) project to the right, a view of the Gulf, as well as the opportunity to receive coastal breezes, is provided.

Mr. Brown needed a big house. Not only did he and his wife have eleven children, but Mrs. Brown had two sisters who lived with them.[1]

Three buildings accompanied the main house. A four-room cottage, located behind the principal house, was occupied by the Browns while the big house was constructed. This building was later used for the kitchen and servants' quarters. Two smaller cottages are located on the front lawn. The building to the west was used as a guest cottage, while the building to the east was Mr. Brown's office and the children's schoolroom.

The bulk of the construction was probably executed by Mr. Brown's laborers from the Madison County plantation. For the finer work, however, carpenters and decorators from New Orleans were imported.[2] The style of the doorway with its abundance of oval glass panes is unique. The design was probably influenced by the setting of the house — overlooking the Gulf of Mexico.

Other unusual features incorporated in the house were the ceiling frescoes and the rounded corners in the central hallway and parlors. The frescoes have been attributed to a German artist named Meuhler.[3]

After Brown's death, the house was sold to Frank Johnston of Jackson (May, 1873), who sold it to Mrs. Sarah A. Dorsey (July, 1873). Mrs. Dorsey, originally from Natchez, named the house Beauvoir, which means beautiful view.

In 1877 Jefferson Davis came to the coast to relax and to write about his experiences. He was invited by Mrs. Dorsey (a friend of Mrs. Davis, who was also from Natchez) to stay at Beauvoir. He rented the east cottage and began writing *The Rise and Fall of the Confederate Government* and *A Short History of the Confederate States.*

During his second year of residency, Mr. Davis contracted to buy Beauvoir. Six months after the first payment was made, Mrs. Dorsey died leaving a will dated the previous year that made Jefferson Davis heir to the house. Mr. Davis lived at Beauvoir for twelve years.

Beauvoir — office and school

After Davis' death in 1889, the property passed to his daughter Winnie. At her death (1898) the house became the property of her mother. Because of failing health and insufficient funds Mrs. Davis sold the house in 1902 to the Mississippi Division Sons of Confederate Veterans with the condition that it be used as a home for former Confederate soldiers and sailors, their wives and widows, orphans, and slaves, as long as there was a need. Mrs. Davis wanted Beauvoir to be a memorial to Jefferson Davis and his family. By 1940 the need for maintaining the home for Confederate soldiers and their families had diminished; hence, Beauvoir was converted into a Jefferson Davis Shrine.

The house is in good condition today and furnished with many pieces used by the Davises. The front portion of the ground floor is used for a Davis Museum. Beauvoir is truly a historic house because of its style of architecture, its construction, and its previous occupants.

Ocean Springs

LOUIS SULLIVAN COTTAGES

Who designed the two bungalows and the octagonal cottage located on East Beach in Ocean Springs — Louis Sullivan or Frank Lloyd Wright? There will probably never be a definite answer to that question. Sullivan wrote that "He planned for two shacks or bungalows, 300 feet apart, with stables far back; also a system of development requiring years for fulfillment."[4] Sullivan's biographer Willard Connely wrote "...they [Sullivan and James Charnley] put their plans, rapidly conceived and sketched as only Sullivan could produce them, into the hands of a local builder."[5] According to Hugh Morrison, "Sullivan designed two bungalows, one for himself and one for the Charnleys, about a hundred yards apart with stables and servants' quarters set far back in the woods. The design of all the buildings was very simple, Sullivan's aim being to make them as inconspicuous as possible in their

Charnley Bungalow and octagonal guest cottage

forest surroundings. The construction was left to a local carpenter. The cottages at Ocean Springs became Sullivan's most-loved home, and for eighteen years he visited them frequently for recreation and the inspiration which he found in a close communion with nature."[6] Frank Lloyd Wright, however, in his biography of Sullivan entitled *The Genius and the Mobocracy*, wrote "He remained away for six weeks at Ocean Springs, Mississippi in the country house I had designed for him." He further commented, "The master was working away in his rose garden down there at Biloxi by the Gulf, next door to his beloved friends the James Charnleys for whom I had drawn a cottage which I liked better than lieber-meister's. Both were experiments that seem tame enough now."[7] Manson in *Frank Lloyd Wright to 1910* questions who designed the cottages and leans toward Wright.[8] Henry Russell Hitchcock[9] attributes the buildings to Wright in his book *In the Nature of Materials 1887–1901* as do Kaufman and Raeburn in their publication *Frank Lloyd Wright: Writings and Buildings*.[10] Storrer will also name Wright as the designer in his forthcoming publication *The Architecture of Frank Lloyd Wright, A Complete Catalog*.[11] If the question of who designed the Sullivan cottages is never answered definitely, we know that they were designed by either of two very famous architects.

Sullivan, considered by many to be the founder of modern architecture, was a partner in the firm Adler and Sullivan in Chicago from 1879 to 1895. The firm's reputation was definitely established after the construction of the Auditorium Building in Chicago 1887–1889. Sullivan, however, became weary from the strain of the important commission. He went to California to relax but found the climate unsuitable. After experiencing a minor earthquake in San Diego he exited immediately for New Orleans where he met friends from Chicago, Mr. and Mrs. James Charnley. Sullivan was displeased with the "filthy conditions" of New Orleans. The Charnleys asked him to go with them to a little hamlet about eighty miles eastward. The exhausted architect enjoyed the natural beauty along the way to the eastern shore of Biloxi Bay. He was delighted with the town which he described as follows:

> With daylight there revealed itself an undulating village all in bloom in softest sunshine, the gentle sparkle of the waters of a bay land-locked by Deer Island; a village sleeping as it had slept for generations with untroubled surface; a people soft-voiced, unconcerned, easy going, indolent; the general store, the post office, the barber shop, the meat market, on Main Street, sheltered by ancient live oaks; the saloon near the depot, the one-man jail in the middle of the street back of the depot; shell roads in the village, wagon trails leading away into the hummock land; no "enterprise," no "progress," no booming for a "Greater Ocean Springs," no factories, no anxious faces, no glare drummers, no white-staked lonely subdivisions. Peace, peace and the joy of comrades, the lovely nights of sea breeze, black pool of the sky oversprinkled with stars brilliant and uncountable.

Continuing, speaking of himself in the third person, Sullivan states: "Here in this haven, this peaceful quiescence, Louis's nerves, long taut with insomnia, yielded and renewed their life. In two weeks he was well and sound."[12]

The Chicago visitors were contacted by Newcomb Clark, a transplanted former Speaker of the House in his home state of Michigan who was living in Ocean Springs for his health. Clark offered to show them some property he would like to sell because "my wife is lonely so far from town; we need neighbors more than trees."[13] Clark showed his property to the Charnleys and Sullivan. Sullivan wrote that he lost his wits when he saw "immense rugged short-leaved pines, sheer eighty feet to their stiff gnarled crowns, graceful swamp pines, very tall, delicately plumed; slender vertical loblolly pines in dense masses; patriarchal sweet gums and black gums with their younger broods; maples, hickories, myrtles; in the undergrowth, dogwoods, Halesias, sloe plums, buckeyes and azaleas, all in a riot of bloom; a giant magnolia and grandiflora near the front — all grouped and arranged as though by the hand of an unseen poet."[14]

James Charnley bought fifteen acres from Newcomb Clark for $750 cash on March 1, 1890.[15] Sullivan purchased six acres in the same section from Mr. and Mrs. Florian Schaffter of New Orleans. He paid $800 on March 7, 1890.[16] Three days later he acquired from Charnley five more acres that adjoined his property for the sum of $1. According to biographer Connely, Charnley was willing to buy the land if Sullivan would design a bungalow for each of them.[17] Whether Sullivan designed the houses for his newly found dreamland or whether he left this up to his draftsman in Chicago, Frank Lloyd Wright, seems to be an unanswerable question. A local builder was responsible for the construction.

The bungalows are T-shaped, shingled structures with steep roofs and long galleries to fend against the sun. The designs for the bungalows are very similar with the elongated front part ending with bay windows for cross ventilation in the bedrooms as well as a view of the Biloxi Bay. The bedrooms are separated by a wide center hall that was used as a comfortable living-dining area. The rear wing contained a hall, a pantry and the kitchen. The wing terminated with an octagonal tower that was used for the tank water supply before the artesian well was dug. The bungalows were probably completed in 1890 or early 1891 at the latest since Sullivan visited his new haven when he came to New Orleans to check on the construction of the Illinois Central Station. An octagonal guest cottage was built for the Charnleys between the bungalows. Servants' quarters, stables, and elaborate rose gardens were completed by June, 1905, since they appeared in an article "The Home of an Artist-Architect" written by Lyndon Smith for *The Architectural Record*.[18] The major emphasis of the article is on the landscaping since Sullivan had developed extensive rose gardens containing approximately a hundred varieties. Both he and his wife Margaret were photographed in various garden settings.

Sullivan's career began to decline after his partnership with Adler was dissolved. Sullivan and his wife reduced their style of living in Chicago but continued to make trips South whenever possible. Eventually money was not available to finance the trips or pay for gardeners to maintain the roses. On August 24, 1905, Sullivan obtained a $5000 loan from Gustav Hottinger, owner of a tile company in Chicago. He pledged his Ocean Springs property for collateral. Sullivan was to repay the money in five years with a five percent per annum service charge.[19] Before the fifth year expired, Hottinger bought the Sullivan property *in toto* on May 1, 1910, for $8500.[20] Sullivan commented, "After eighteen years of tender care, the paradise, the poem of spring, Sullivan's other self, was wrecked by a wayward West Indies hurricane."[21]

The Hottinger family owned the property for thirty-three years. On March 6, 1943, William G. Nichols of Birmingham, Alabama, became the owner of Sullivan's former paradise.[22] After Mr. Nichols' death the property was acquired by Monsignor Gregory R. Kennedy and his sister Miss Kathleen Kennedy on April 5, 1968. The Kennedys altered the structure by adding a room to the front of the house. They enclosed the property with a chain link fence. Today there are no roses. Suffice it to say the character of the house and grounds have changed considerably and no longer fit the description provided by Lyndon Smith.

The Charnleys kept their Ocean Springs property for six years and then sold it to Lizzie W. Norwood, also of Chicago. The house burned but was rebuilt following the original plans. The only change made in the house was the interior walls were finished with beautiful curly pine.[23]

In 1911 the Norwoods sold the property which continued to change hands several times and was once used briefly as a night club before Mr. Leslie C. Wiswell of Chicago rescued the house. The Wiswells removed the paint and beer posters from the curly pine walls. They also enlarged the narrow porch on the east side of the rear wing.

After Mr. Wiswell died, Mrs. Wiswell sold the property to Mr. and Mrs. Stanley P. Ruddiman in two parts with the first transaction occurring July 12, 1954, and the second June 1, 1963.[24] The present owners are the sons of Stanley Ruddiman who purchased the property from their parents. Mr. and Mrs. Edsel Ruddiman own and occupy the bungalow while Mr. Bill Ruddiman has the guest cottage.

ST. JOHN'S EPISCOPAL CHURCH

Several writers have attributed the design of St. John's Episcopal Church to Louis Sullivan. Willard Connely wrote that Sullivan designed the unassuming church without a steeple. Local residents decided the church looked too much like a chapel; therefore, after Sullivan left town, they added the steeple.[25] Other critics of Sullivan's work have not mentioned the Episcopal Church.

The church records indicate that the design for the church was obtained from a church magazine. Further research is needed to identify the source for the design of the picturesque structure.

St. John's Episcopal Church

Gautier

The little town of Gautier, located on the west bank of the Pascagoula River between Biloxi and Pascagoula, has two interesting houses: Old Place Plantation House and Oldfields.

OLD PLACE PLANTATION HOUSE

The French cottage was designed and constructed (1856) by Fernando Upton Gautier for his wife, to last "as long as his love." The house is distinctly French, with its slender colonettes and broad galleries surrounding the house. French doors, especially adaptable for the coastal climate, were used on each corner of the house. When the windows and ten doors are open, breezes flow easily through the house.

The floorplan for the house is unusual, with the double parlors being a long room that separates four bedrooms. A breezeway connects the

Old Place Plantation House

house to a similar building, with a hip roof and spacious galleries, which contains the kitchen and dining room. The kitchen is one of the most authentic kitchens in the state, with its many antique utensils and a massive fireplace. One is reminded that the occupants were French when the labels on the canisters are read. The spacious dining room has a punkah over the dining room table.

Gautier's Plantation House has always belonged to the Gautier family, and it still contains the original, very fine quality furnishings. The house is open to the public.

OLDFIELDS

Oldfields, which is similar in style to The Briars in Natchez, was built by Mr. Alfred Lewis who owned vast acreage in the area. The house is located on a bluff overlooking the Pascagoula River. Many windows and doors open onto the eighty-five foot gallery. The second floor has a spacious ballroom.

Oldfields

Pascagoula

LONGFELLOW HOUSE

Longfellow House, also known as Bellevue and Pollock Place, is a mid-nineteenth-century house with an exposed stuccoed basement. The house contains black marble mantels, ceilings decorated with plaster medallions, and a spiral stairway. The house was constructed for a Mr. and Mrs. Graham, slave traders from New Orleans.

The house, once used for a girls' school, has had a long list of owners, including people from Maine, Missouri, Louisiana, and Moss Point and Greenville, Mississippi. W. A. Pollock, a planter and banker of Greenville and New Orleans owned the house for the longest period of time, 1902–1938. The house is now owned by Ingalls Shipbuilding Corporation and is used as a tourist resort.

Legend has it that the poet Henry Wadsworth Longfellow, staying at Bellevue shortly after it was constructed, was inspired to write the poem "The Building of the Ship," which contains the reference "from Pascagoula's sunny bay." The house is known today as the Longfellow House.

Longfellow House

Spanish Fort

SPANISH FORT

The oldest building featured in this publication is known as the Old Spanish Fort (1718) which is a misnomer since the building was probably constructed by Joseph Simon de la Pointe, a French Naval Officer who came to the Gulf Coast with D'Iberville and Bienville in 1699. Around 1730 a German named Hugo Ernestus Krebs came to the area and later married de la Pointe's daughter, Marie Josephine. Hence the Spanish Fort is sometimes referred to as Krebs Fort. The Spanish Fort title was appropriate around 1766 when the Spaniards moved into Pascagoula to take over from the British who had taken over from the French six years previously. After the Spanish Fort was used as a military post it later became a residence. Since 1949 the building has been maintained as a museum by the Jackson County Historical Society.

The National Park Service was responsible for having measured drawings made of the building in 1940. The data sheet indicates the oldest part of the building (the central section) is built of cypress and cedar frame filled in with oyster shell cement. The first addition was built on the east side utilizing oyster shell cement again. The room on the west end however, is frame filled with a bouzillage of clay and moss. The National Park surveyors concluded: "This structure is probably the oldest by some years of any standing between the Appalachians and the Rocky Mountains. It is a great archaeological curiosity and a unique survival from the earliest period of Gulf Coast colonization."

In 1971 the Spanish Fort was listed on the National Register of Historic Places. The Jackson County Historical Society has studied the history of the building and has obtained appropriate relics for the museum.

FREDERIC HOUSE

According to the Jackson County Genealogical Society, the Frederic House was built in 1829 by Louis Augustus Frederic, a Frenchman, who was twice knighted for bravery by Napoleon Bonaparte. Frederic's med-

Frederic House —original section behind 1895 addition

als are housed in the Spanish Fort museum. In Pascagoula, Frederic was the postmaster and schoolmaster.

The Frederic house is at the rear of the 1895 addition. The original structure contains four downstairs rooms with a center hallway. One large room, which was the schoolroom, is upstairs. The first shutters were solid instead of slatted.

NOTES TO PART THREE

1. Martha Bassett, "History of Beauvoir, 1949—1969," M.A. thesis, University of Southern Mississippi, 1970.

2. Gulf Coast Chapters of the Mississippi Division United Daughters of the Confederacy, *Beauvoir—Jefferson Davis Shrine* (1968), p. 3.

3. *Ibid.*, p. 14.

4. Louis H. Sullivan, *The Autobiography of An Idea* (New York: W. W. Norton & Company, Inc. 1924), p. 297.

5. William Connely, *Louis Sullivan As He Lived* (New York: Horizon Press, Inc. 1960), p. 125.

6. Hugh Morrison, *Louis Sullivan* (New York: W. W. Norton & Company, Inc., 1962), p. 112.

7. Frank Lloyd Wright, *The Genius and the Mobocracy* (New York: Horizon Press, 1949), p. 67.

8. Grant Carpenter Manson, *Frank Lloyd Wright to 1910* (New York: Reinhold Publishing Corporation, 1958), pp. 24-25.

9. Henry Russell Hitchcock, *In the Nature of Materials—The Buildings of Frank Lloyd Wright, 1887—1941* (New York: Duell, Sloan and Pearce, 1942), p. 108.

10. Edgar Kaufmann and Ben Raeburn, *Frank Lloyd Wright: Writings and Buildings* (New York: Horizon Press, 1960), p. 335.

11. William Allin Storrer, personal letter to Margaret Steelman, February 15, 1971.

12. Sullivan, p. 295.

13. *Ibid.*, p. 296.

14. *Ibid.*, p. 297.

15. Jackson County, Mississippi, *Warranty Deed Book,* number 11, p. 13.

16. Jackson County, Mississippi, *Warranty Deed Book,* number 11, p. 44.

17. Connely, p. 125.

18. Lyndon Smith, "The Home of an Artist Architect," *The Architectural Record,* June, 1905.

19. Jackson County, Mississippi, *Deed of Trust Book,* number 2, pp. 143-144.

20. Jackson County, Mississippi, *Warranty Deed Book,* number 35, pp. 600-602.

21. Sullivan, p. 297.

22. Jackson County, Mississippi, *Warranty Deed Book,* number 82, pp. 481-483.

23. Ray Thompson, "East Beach of Ocean Springs Takes a Bow," *Know Your Coast,* July 29, 1957, p. 2.

24. Jackson County, Mississippi, *Warranty Deed Book,* number 234, p. 537.

25. Connely, p. 239.

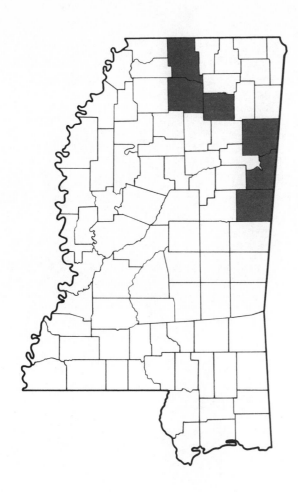

Macon

Macon, Columbus, and Aberdeen developed soon after the Choctaws ceded their land to the United States. Macon, located south of Columbus, was incorporated in 1836. The town is situated near the Noxubee and Tombigbee rivers. The Jackson Military Road, another major traffic artery, passed through this area.

Four houses were selected to be representative of the early architecture of Macon: the Cline House is a cottage; Belle Oakes is an early mansion type (1844); the Harrison House is a later, more decorated mansion type; and the Flora Residence was built in 1868. The treatment of the front door is similar in all four houses, with emphasis on the vertical rather than the horizontal line. That is, in most Greek Revival doorways the transom lights span the door and the side lights and are frequently surmounted by a cornice. In the Macon houses, however, most of the doors have only three transom lights while the side lights extend beyond the height of the door to the top of the transom lights. The floor-length windows maintain the vertical emphasis and are oftentimes accented with side lights. Doric columns predominate.

CLINE HOUSE

Ownership of the Cline House has remained in the family of the builder-designer, Logan Cline. The house consists of four rooms and a large central hallway downstairs, with two unfinished rooms upstairs. The typical Macon door is outlined with Greek Revival millwork. The closed shutters conceal the triple-hung, floor-length windows.

Cline House

Belle Oakes

BELLE OAKES

The most imposing mansion in Macon is Belle Oakes, constructed in 1844 for Judge Hampton Lee Jarnigen. The house is built on a grand scale — with ceilings fourteen feet high, rooms that measure twenty feet square, and an unusual stairway that dominates the entrance hall. The flying-wing stairway is modified by a supplementary stairway that leads to the rear of the second-floor hall while the main stairway leads to the front of the hall. The parlor and dining room contain a white marble mantel and a ceiling ornamented with plasterwork.

The facade of the massive Greek Revival structure has been slightly altered since a ground level brick floor has been substituted for the original raised wooden floor which was outlined by a balustrade. The wide plank steps that extended the full width between the two interior Doric columns have been deleted, as well as the solarium that was located to the left of the library.

The front gallery has a paneled ceiling, a balcony supported by iron brackets, and the typical Macon door treatment consisting of three transom lights and tall side lights. The windows on the lower level are eleven feet tall and extend to the floor. The windows are further accented by slender side lights and shutters.

HARRISON HOUSE

Romantic tendencies are evident in the architecture of this house built for W. W. Goodwin around 1855. Note the octagonal columns, the decorative balustrade, the arched windows, and the side porches. An ell with service rooms is attached to the right rear of the house, and

Harrison House

the original kitchen is a detached brick structure. At one time the house contained a fine stairway with a gentle curve from left to right, marble mantels, decorative plaster moldings, and a third-story observatory. The house has been used as a residence, a school, and now as an antique shop.

FLORA RESIDENCE

John Lee Williams built his stately mansion in 1868. The structure was probably even more imposing in earlier years when the flat roof was topped by a cupola. The design, number, and arrangement of fenestrations make them the dominate feature of the facade. The doorway treatment is repeated in the windows with the tall, floor-length windows framed with sidelights. The original bifold shutters are still used to block the late afternoon sun. The balcony, supported by iron brackets, is one of the loveliest in the state. This house also has marble mantels, decorative plasterwork, and a cantilevered stairway. Folding doors separate the double parlors.

Flora Residence

Columbus

Columbus, located on the bluffs of the Tombigbee River in northeast Mississippi, was incorporated in 1821. Since the Tombigbee River was navigable to Mobile and General Jackson's Military Road extended from Nashville to New Orleans via Columbus, the area was easily accessible. The population did not increase rapidly, however, until the early 1830s when the Choctaw and Chickasaw Indians ceded their land to the

Mississippi State College for Women

First Methodist Church

Catholic Church of the Annunciation

United States government. Many families from Tennessee, Georgia, Virginia, and the Carolinas flocked to the Columbus land office to buy the good prairie soil for about two dollars per acre.[1]

Education and religion received attention early in the history of Columbus. Franklin Academy, the oldest public school in Mississippi, was established here in 1821. In addition several private schools for women preceded the establishment of the nation's first state supported college for women in Columbus in 1884 (Photo).

Columbus has many fine churches. The First Methodist Church, the Catholic Church of the Annunciation and the Episcopal Church are three of the oldest and most significant from the standpoint of architecture. The two-story brick Methodist Church with a towering spire was started around 1860 and completed except for the basement in 1867. Colonel T. C. Billups was chairman of the building committee. Construction of the Catholic Church also began in the 1860s, with Father Mouton, who belonged to the Order of Architects in the Catholic Church, given credit for the design of this architectural gem.

Saint Paul's Episcopal Church, completed in 1858, is noteworthy because of its pointed gothic style and a Tiffany window. The window is stamped in the lower right hand corner with the date 1899 and the name Tiffany Decorating Company of New York. To the right of the church is the Victorian rectory that was constructed between 1876 and 1880.[2] Tennessee Williams, noted playwright, was born in Columbus in 1911 and lived in the rectory for three years while his grandfather, Walter E. Dakin, was the rector of the Episcopal church.[3]

The Lowndes County Courthouse was constructed in 1847 according to a classic design developed by architect James S. Lull who came to

Tiffany window   Saint Paul's Episcopal Church

Columbus from Vermont. The facade of the courthouse was changed in 1901 by architect R. H. Hunt of Chattanooga.

Columbians elected to build town houses rather than plantation houses. These houses, usually two-storied with Greek Revival influences predominating, often occupied a full city block with their detached

Lowndes County Courthouse — constructed in 1847, facade changed in 1901

Episcopal Rectory—first home of playwright Tennessee Williams

kitchens, carriage houses, service buildings, orchards, and vegetable gardens.

Some typical features included in the Columbus houses are: roof capped with a cupola, tower or belvedere; square paneled columns on the earlier houses, octagonal columns on the later houses; doorways with rectangular transom lights and side lights (often of Venetian glass); fine interior millwork with the Greek Revival key or crossette pattern predominating; elaborate, very fine quality plaster medallions and cornices; marble mantels, usually white but in some houses black; and spectacular staircases that dominate the entrance hall.

A style of architecture that appears to be unique to the Columbus area combines Gothic and Italianate detail with the Greek Revival plan (see Themerlaine, Errolton, and Shadowlawn). The "bracketed mode," which was promoted by the writings of Andrew Downing was also very popular. Columbus still has approximately one hundred ante-bellum houses. Many of the houses and buildings were used to shelter the wounded after the Battle of Shiloh in April, 1862.[4]

The Cedars — log construction exposed in the parlor

THE CEDARS

One of the older houses in Columbus is The Cedars. The house encompasses a three-room log cabin that may date as early as 1810.

The Cedars

One wall of the pioneer construction has been exposed in the living room (Photo). The Cedars was enlarged in 1839 by Captain Edward Brett Randolph who came to Mississippi from Virginia.

Another house in Columbus that contains a log structure is Hickory Sticks.

Several of the older homes in Columbus can be classified as raised cottages. This style of architecture is usually associated with low-lying areas, such as New Orleans. However, at least five raised cottages can be seen in Columbus with the Pratt Thomas Home being the most elegant.

PRATT THOMAS HOME

The Pratt Thomas Home, built around 1833 by Scotsman Adolphus B. Weir who came to this area to represent the government at the Indian land sales, is a raised cottage with the lower level constructed of brick,

Pratt Thomas Home

while the second floor is of wood. Since the upper level is the main floor, it has taller ceilings and finer millwork.

The second floor is emphasized by the "welcoming arms" stairway and the decorative columns. The grooved columns with Ionic capitals, the pilasters, and the typical Greek Revival doorway arrangement were probably the first architectural orders in Columbus.

The floor plan includes a cross hall that parallels the recessed gallery and leads to spacious bedrooms at each end. This hall is especially attractive. Its walls are covered with antique Zuber mural wallpaper. The room has a warm glow in the afternoon as the sunlight is filtered

Pratt Thomas Home — rear view. Small brick building is original kitchen.

by the amber-colored, etched Venetian glass located on each side and above the doorway. The door has a silver knob and bell.

Double parlors with black marble mantels are located behind the cross hall. The back gallery, enhanced with iron grillwork, has been glassed in for year-around comfort, while retaining the original architectural features (Photo). The dining room was located on the first level for easy access from the detached kitchen, which still exists in the rear yard (Photo).

Only three families have owned the elegant raised cottage. Mr. Weir, the builder, sold the house in 1850 to Richard Sykes, who twenty years later sold it to Colonel William C. Richards. The house has remained in the Richards family over one hundred years, with the present owner being Colonel Richards' granddaughter — Mrs. Pratt Thomas.

The grounds are beautifully landscaped with camellias, azaleas, boxwoods, and native greenery all enclosed with a brick and iron fence. The many bricks were obtained from the Confederate arsenal, which was destroyed by fire.

LEHMQUEN

Two houses that were built about the same time and have similar features are Lehmquen and Twelve Gables. Lehmquen, a story-and-a-half structure enclosed by an exquisite iron fence, has Doric columns, corner block millwork, transom and side lights around the front door, and two large dormers with double windows to light the upstairs bedrooms.

The center hallway is dominated by a flying-wing stairway that begins just to the right of the left parlor door and curves to the right. The plaster cornice in the hall and parlor is especially deep and handsome,

Lehmquen

Twelve Gables — note ashlar pattern on facade

while the interior woodwork repeats the corner block design of the facade. The door knobs and keyhole covers at Lehmquen are silver. The original kitchen may have been in one of the two large rooms in the basement.

TWELVE GABLES

Twelve Gables has two distinctive features: its many gables — five across the front and back and two at each end — and its facade that has an ashlar design cut into the thick planks. The floor plan consists of four rooms on the principal floor divided by a wide central hallway with a flying-wing stair; two rooms and a hall are upstairs. The original kitchen is in the basement.

The John Morton family lived in Twelve Gables for several generations. In April, 1866, Miss Matt Morton, daughter of John Morton, was one of the founders of Decoration Day. She and her friends decided to decorate the graves of the Civil War dead, both friend and foe, that were buried in Friendship Cemetery. According to tradition, this event was planned in the parlor of Twelve Gables. The gesture was recorded by F. M. Finch in a poem entitled "The Blue and the Gray" that was published in *The Atlantic Monthly* in September, 1867.

TEMPLE HEIGHTS

Temple Heights was built for Richard T. Brownrigg who was a member of the North Carolina state legislature before moving to Lowndes county in 1836 with his wife, Mary W. Hoskins, and their five children. He purchased extensive acreage and a house in the prairie that had belonged to John Pitchlyn, Choctaw Indian Chief and interpreter. Brownrigg, who had studied medicine but never practiced, was one of the founders of the town of West Port on the west side of the Tombigbee river and was owner of the ferry which linked West Port to Columbus. He soon became very active in church and educational affairs in Columbus (i.e. first senior warden for St. Paul's Episcopal Church, a member of the board of trustees for the Mississippi Female

Temple Heights — original front

Temple Heights—facade changed around mid-nineteenth century by adding 10 columns.

College that was established in Columbus in 1838) and, consequently, decided a town house would be more convenient for him and his family. Therefore, around 1839 he started the construction of a town house on one of the highest bluffs in Columbus. His Mississippi home utilized a floor plan that was more typical of the town houses along the Atlantic seaboard with each of the four levels having two rooms and a hall.[5] The original facade, which faces south, features an exposed basement, four two-story Doric columns, and a balcony. The exterior chimneys are on the west side of the house since the hall runs the length of the east side. The mantels on the principal floor are of black marble. The millwork is of the corner block design and the doors have a painted grain. The large locks on the hall doors were made by the British firm of Carpenter and Company, which manufactured locks from 1820 to 1835. Brownrigg died in December, 1846. The following year Temple Heights was sold for $3,350 at public auction to Thomas W. Harris, a statesman from Georgia. Harris was a probate judge for Lowndes County and a wealthy planter (according to the 1860 census, his real estate was valued at forty thousand dollars while his personal estate was valued at sixty thousand).

Wanting a more impressive residence, Harris changed the town house appearance to look more like a Greek temple by adding two galleries and ten columns and ornamenting the frieze with triglyphs. The east facade became "the front."

When Harris died, his son sold the house to his wife's sister, Mrs. Francis Jane Butler Fontaine, who was one of the ladies who initiated the celebration of Decoration Day (see Twelve Gables). In 1887 Mrs. Fontaine sold the house for $2,600 to the J. H. Kennebrew family who retained ownership for seventy-eight years. Mrs. Kennebrew wanted to be sure that her five daughters would always have a home; therefore, she stipulated in her will that Temple Heights should not be sold until all her daughters were married. Two of the daughters never married. By 1965 the house was in a sad state of disrepair. To save the structure, Mr. Kirk Egger bought the house and then sold it three years later to Mr. and Mrs. Carl Butler who restored the edifice as an elegant town house once again.

Whitehall

HOMEWOOD AND WHITEHALL

Homewood and Whitehall are two early wooden mansions that have similar features with each house having six paneled square columns; a hip roof; six-over-six double-hung windows, formally placed; a balcony; dentils; and colored glass side lights around a typical Greek Revival doorway. Homewood has millwork that is grooved and accented with corner blocks. The house, one of the first "big" houses in Columbus, was built for Mr. W. M. Cozart. Homewood has been occupied by members of the J. T. Wood family since 1894.

Whitehall (1843) was built approximately seven years after Homewood and is more decorated. The hip roof is capped with a belvedere; pilasters are placed between the windows; and the chimney tops are corbeled. The house was built for Judge James Walton Harris, a prominent planter who came to Columbus from Georgia.

Both houses have original service buildings located in the rear yards.

Homewood

117

Vernacular architecture in Columbus is exemplified by Themerlaine, Errolton, and Shadowlawn. These houses (along with two others that were destroyed) combine Greek and Gothic Revival features in a way that is unique to the Columbus area. The two-story columns, formal floor plan, and symmetrical arrangement of fenestrations represent the Greek style, while the octagonal form of the columns, the wooden tracery, and the side porches are more picturesque Gothic features. The five houses were similar in design yet still very individualistic.

THEMERLAINE

Themerlaine is an imposing three-story structure that appears even larger than its grand scale since it is located on a hill and boasts two porticoes — one for access from the street and one for carriage arrival. The entries are flanked by pilasters and Venetian glass side lights. The entry from the street side leads into a hallway that divides double parlors. The parlors have decorative plaster medallions and cornices, matching marble mantels, and both jib and sliding doors. The entry from the side leads into a long hall that passes the front hall, thus forming a T. This hallway contains the staircase and also separates a bedroom and the dining room from the parlors. Four bedrooms are located upstairs; the original kitchen and servant quarters were on the first floor.

Themerlaine

When Elias Fort built Themerlaine in 1844, the house was located on a six-acre site that contained formal flower gardens, orchards, vegetable gardens, a carriage house, well house, and smokehouse. Fort was a planter from North Carolina who established a plantation near Columbus.

Errolton

Errolton — decorative ceiling and cornice

ERROLTON

Tudor arches with wooden tracery spandrels decorate the expanse between octagonal columns at Errolton. The typical Greek Revival doorway with pilasters and dentils has side and transom lights of red glass to filter and warm the northern light while blue glass is used around the rear entry to cool the sunlight from the south.

Elegant double parlors with marble mantels are located to the right of the central hallway. Plaster medallions in the acanthus-leaf pattern decorate the center of each ceiling, and a deep cornice of molded plaster outlines the walls. Pier mirrors are placed between the jib doors at each end of the parlors. A continuous, gold-leaf cornice stretches over the windows and the mirror. The chandeliers reflect into infinity.

SHADOWLAWN

Shadowlawn was constructed in 1860 by Hardy Stevens for John W. Spears, a merchant. This house combines Italianate features with the Greek form. The formal floor plan, low roof, two-story columns, doorway and interior details are basically Greek while the rounded arches formed by wooden tracery, the brackets under the eaves and the side porch are Italianate features.

Shadowlawn

Colonnade and Snowdoun are also mansion-type structures that contain both Greek and Gothic features.

COLONNADE

Colonnade is approximately the same age as Shadowlawn and also possesses several romantic tendencies — the asymmetrical placement of the door, the jigsaw balcony balustrade, and the deep brackets. The floor plan is a short T, with the off-center hallway, parlor, and a bedroom forming the central section of the house. A bedroom and porch are located to the left, while the dining room and porch are to the right.

Colonnade

Two bedrooms and a large hall are upstairs. The original kitchen and storage room are behind the house and are presently used for a playroom and utility area.

The house was built for William T. Baldwin, a planter from Georgia. The red glass around the front entry is not original, but it is appropriate. The panes came from the Keeler house when it was demolished. Colonnade was built on a grand scale, with a ceiling height of fourteen feet and rooms measuring twenty-two feet square. The parlor has floor-length windows and a white marble mantel.

SNOWDOUN

The design of Snowdoun combines Greek and Gothic motifs with the octagonal form. The octagonal form was incorporated in many houses in Columbus, with Snowdoun, Waverley, and White Arches using it most extensively. According to family tradition, Governor James Whitfield, a banker and builder of Snowdoun, was influenced in his house design by a visit he made to Jefferson's Monticello, which features an octagonal cupola. Originally the octagonal stairwell at Snow-

Snowdoun

doun was surmounted by an octagonal cupola. The cupola was removed in later years and a gable roof added when the original roof began to leak.

Four square rooms open off the octagonal stairwell. The square shape is obtained by incorporating triangular shaped closets. A winding stairway rises from the left side of the stairwell and spirals up to the cupola. Four bedrooms are upstairs. The house has marble mantels, plaster ceiling decorations, and Venetian glass side lights. Snowdoun was built in 1854. The design is attributed to William H. O'Neal, an architect originally from North Carolina.

The irregular floor plan has seven porches with decorative jigsaw balustrades. Access to many of the porches is by jib doors. Local historians have recorded that Jefferson Davis made a speech during his campaign for the U.S. Senate from the front balcony at Snowdoun.

The house was purchased in the 1860s by John M. Billups, who was a planter and a banker. In 1860, according to the Census, Billups was thirty-six years old, a Georgian, and owner of real estate valued at $60,000 and personal assets of $314,000. Snowdoun has remained the property of his family.

The original brick kitchen is located behind the house and was once connected by a covered walkway. Since the house faces a corner, the gallery can be approached from two sides. A formal, oval-shaped garden is laid out in front of the house.

Columbus has many bracketed cottages that are similar in design to those promoted by Andrew Jackson Downing in his writings. The Amzi Love house may be considered as the representative for this group.

AMZI LOVE HOUSE

Amzi Love, a young lawyer, built a bracketed cottage for his bride, Edith. The picturesque structure with arches and openwork columns gradually shifted from the category of being a "honeymoon cottage" to being the home of a young couple with five daughters and a son. Seven generations of the Love family have occupied the cottage, keeping it and its furnishings essentially the same as Amzi and Edith planned them.

The entrance to the cottage is especially attractive with diamond-shaped panes of Venetian glass in blue, red, green, and yellow framing a massive, paneled door. The door has different styles of paneling on the exterior and interior surfaces.

A gracefully curved stairway dominates the entrance hall. Its handrail, decorative balusters, and unusual S–shaped newel post are of walnut. Beneath the stairway is located the only closet in the house. It is neatly camouflaged by decorative paneling. Armoires and chests are used even today for storage.

To the left of the central hallway is the parlor, which contains jib doors, the original furnishings, chandelier and cornices. The wood mantel is decorated with bas relief. The present owner, Mrs. Edith Wallace McGeorge Woodward, who is a member of the fifth generation of the Love family, says "It seems we never sold anything nor gave anything away!" Since the family never moved to another dwelling, many items that would probably have been discarded were saved;

Amzi Love House

therefore, the Amzi Love house is a great place for historical research and for viewing interesting collections.

Three small buildings that were probably built about the same time as the cottage are located behind the house. One building was the smokehouse for meat, the second was the dairy house, where water from an artesian well flowed through to keep the dairy products cool, and the third was the privy. The original detached kitchen was attached to the house many years ago. Today the house is in excellent condition and is especially attractive in the spring when the massive azaleas are in bloom.

FRANKLIN SQUARE

Franklin Square

All of the houses mentioned so far have been constructed of wood. Columbus also has some fine brick structures. Franklin Square is one of the oldest brick houses in Columbus (1835). The house was purchased in the 1870s by Sidney Franklin who added the south facade and altered the stairway. The pediments are supported by paired columns and ornamented with a decorative iron grille. Formal gardens are laid out to the west of the house which is still occupied by descendents of Sidney Franklin.

STEPHEN D. LEE HOME

A house that has special meaning for many Columbians is the Stephen D. Lee Home. The building was used as a part of Lee High School for many years and presently houses a museum and serves as headquarters for historic societies. The house, now listed on the National Register for Historic Buildings, was built in 1847 for Major Thomas Garton Blewett. The Major planned the house with generous dimensions; for example, the parlor measures 30 feet by forty feet. A bedroom wing and a conservatory were removed from the building when the building was used for classrooms. The severity of the architec-

Stephen D. Lee Home

Stephen D. Lee Home — detail of iron work

tural features are softened somewhat on the exterior by the lacy iron grillwork and on the interior by decorative plasterwork.

The house became the property of Blewett's granddaughter who married the distinguished Confederate General, Stephen D. Lee. In 1880, General Lee became the first president of Mississippi State Agricultural and Mechanical College.

Two of the finest buildings in Columbus are the brick structures named Camellia Place and Riverview. The design for these houses, as well as several other buildings in Columbus, is attributed by local tradition to James S. Lull, an architect who was born in Vermont. It is thought that Lull probably built Camellia Place for himself and his wife and then enlarged and embellished the plan for Mr. and Mrs. Charles McLaran who named their place Riverview. The houses do have many similar features: two main stories surmounted by a cupola; front porticoes supported by four square paneled columns; cornices accented with dentils; windows alternated with engaged columns or pilasters which create a feeling of stability as well as rhythm; and magnificent spiral stairways that reach from the rear of the central hallways to the fourth-floor cupolas.

CAMELLIA PLACE

Although Camellia Place is older than Riverview, it looks more recent when viewed from the inside, since the interior is an excellent example of a Greek Revival house "remodeled" during the Victorian period.

Mrs. Eugenia Morgan Moore (great aunt of the present owner, John Morgan Kaye) purchased Camellia Place in 1884 from the Lull heirs. Desiring to update her almost forty-year-old Greek Revival house, Mrs. Moore went to Chicago to purchase Victorian furnishings and architectual elements. She bought tall marble and onyx mantels with mirror insets, custom-designed mahogany woodwork, and a cherry handrail for the spectacular stair that loops to the fourth-floor observa-

Camellia Place

Camellia Place — hallway detail. Victorian millwork added in 1884.

tory (Photo). The house and the furnishings remain today very much as "Aunt Eugenia" planned them.

Many specimen camellia plants grow on the surrounding grounds. Consequently, the name Camellia Place is appropriate. The house and grounds are enclosed by an attractive iron fence.

RIVERVIEW

The most imposing house in Columbus is Riverview — a four story, brick structure that has matching front and rear facades for an attractive approach from either the street or the river. The stately mansion was built for Colonel and Mrs. Charles McLaran. Mrs. McLaran died, however, before the house was finished. Riverview was completed and furnished except for permanent chandeliers by November 27, 1852. An article in *The Southern Standard,* a Columbus newspaper, described a large scale party that Colonel McLaran hosted "on Thursday and Friday evenings of last week'' for his numerous friends in the city and vicinity. The cast iron animals that guard the Riverview entry and grace the grounds were in place for the 1852 party according to the newspaper account which also describes the house and the guests.

To describe Riverview is a challenge because of its size and the many architectural details. Riverview is the largest antebellum house in north Mississippi with its three-room-deep floor plan. (Natchez has three

Riverview — The closed shutters on Riverview serve as reminders of the importance of symmetry in Greek Revival buildings. The exterior design called for alternating windows with pilasters at regular intervals. The closed shutters only suggest windows since they actually conceal a chimney which was needed for the front room.

houses that are three rooms deep: Melrose, Stanton Hall and Brandon Hall.) The brick structure has a basement; six rooms, and two hallways on the principal floor; bedrooms and ballrooms on the second floor; storage space on the third level; and a view of Columbus and the Tombigbee River from the fourth floor, nineteen-foot-square observatory.

The entrance hall contains architectural features that require Riverview to be referred to as a mansion rather than just a house. For exam-

Riverview — scenic side lights parallel the second story door that opens onto the front balcony. Similar glass probably appeared around the other entries originally.

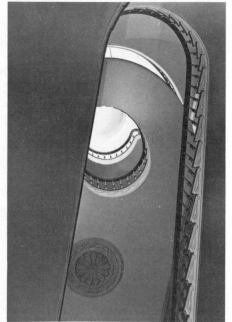

Riverview — spectacular stairway that loops to the fourth floor cupola

Riverview — plaster medallion in original dining room

ple, the central hallway contains a curved stairway that loops up to the cupola (Photo). Natural light is provided in the stairwell by the twelve windows with stained glass panes in the cupola. The ceiling for the front part of the hall is enhanced with a plaster medallion composed of acanthus leaves and rosettes. The egg-and-dart motif outline the radial design of the coffered ceiling (Photo). Greek Revival millwork, decorative plaster cornices, an S-shaped newel post and a niche for statuary complete the hallway decoration. The paneled doors behind the stairway conceal the back hall that contains a service stair.

Double parlors are located to the right of the central hallway. These spacious rooms have black marble mantels and fourteen-foot ceilings that are embellished with the finest plasterwork in the state (Photo). The parlors can be separated by sliding doors. An anteroom is located behind the back parlor. Three rooms — library, dining room, and bedroom — are located on the left side of the hallway. The library and dining room can be separated by a paneled wooden wall that operates vertically. The dining room has an exterior side door for easy access from the original detached kitchen. These rooms also have marble mantels and plaster medallions. The second floor room arrangement is the same as the first floor with ball rooms above the parlors and bedrooms on the opposite side.

McLaran, who was a planter, sold the house in 1857 to Mr. John Gilmer, owner of the Gilmer Hotel and a member of the state legislature. He is known as an early advocate of women's rights. Captain W. W. Humphries, a lawyer, was the next owner. He and his descendants owned the property for the longest period 1881–1965. To rescue the house from possible demolition or alteration, Mr. and Mrs. Pratt Thomas bought stately Riverview which is across the street from their elegant home. Six years later the house was sold to Dr. and Mrs. John Murfee who are dedicated historians and civic leaders.

Columbus has two excellent examples of Italianate design in Rosedale and White Arches. Some typical Italianate features incorporated

Riverview — ceiling detail in foyer

Riverview—plasterwork in double parlors

into both houses are rounded arches, a flat roof, a tower (reminiscent of a campanile), slender octagonal colonettes, canopies supported by curved rafters, and balconies with iron grillwork.

ROSEDALE

Rosedale, constructed of brick and then stuccoed, was built for Dr. William Topp around 1855. The architectural beauty can easily be appreciated, since the house is located in a pastoral setting. The trees around Rosedale attest to Andrew Jackson Downing's belief that "a

Rosedale

building in this style will be greatly heightened in effect by being well supported by trees, the irregular forms of which will harmonize with the character of the architecture."[6]

The Italianate manner of Rosedale is emphasized by Venetian arch windows on each side of the third-floor tower, by brackets underneath the wide eaves, by a canopy projecting over the balcony, and by the use of decorative wooden tracery.

WHITE ARCHES

White Arches has several features that give the house individuality. For example, the facade is dominated by an octagonal tower that rises for three stories and is then capped with a belvedere. The tower contains two stairways to make the ascent to the belvedere possible. The tower is supported by four substantial pillars that may appear to be paneled from a distance. Upon closer examination, however (Photo of column), one notices that the pillars are a cluster of four octagonal posts. The slender colonettes that support the canopy repeat the octagonal form.

Another unusual feature found in White Arches is the number and design of the doors. There are seven exterior doors on the first floor and eight on the second level. Most of the doors are double doors with glass panes and decorative side lights of etched stain or satin glass. For a safety feature, the double doors that open onto the galleries and balconies have a door knob only on the interior side. The galleries are outlined with decorative wood, and the balconies are outlined with iron banisters. Brass finials are used at the corners of the iron rails.

The floor plan of the White Arches includes a central hallway with the parlor and dining room to the right. These rooms contain matching marble mantels, decorative cornices, and ceiling medallions. Sliding doors can be used to separate the rooms. To the left of the central hall is a library with elegant built-in bookcases of walnut. This room also has a marble mantel; etched frosted glass side lights; ceiling rosette; and random-width pine floors, with each board running the full length of the room. The library is separated from the bedroom by a cross hall that leads from a side entrance into the center hall. The center hall contains the main staircase, made of mahogany, while a back stairway is located in the small hall behind the center hall. This back stair, which has a graceful curve, makes the four bedrooms on the upper floor more accessible. The bedrooms house yet another unusual feature —closets.

Behind the house are located brick buildings that were used for the kitchen, laundry room, and storage area. A carriage house, now gone, was at the rear of the block.

White Arches was planned in 1857 for Jeptha Vining Harris, a Georgian, who came to Mississippi shortly after he had married Mary Oliver Banks in 1840. His family had been active in politics in Georgia, and by 1856 he was a member of the Mississippi state legislature. Ultimately, he became a wealthy planter and a brigadier general in the Confederate army.

The Harrises hosted one of the last of the old time parties at White Arches when they had a debut party for Miss Mary Oliver Harris. The party was held the night before the Columbus riflemen left for war.

White Arches — note the curved rafters and the octagonal columns and colonettes

White Arches

White Arches could easily accommodate a large-scale party with its spacious halls, the parlor and dining room that opened into an area forty feet long, and the double doors that opened onto the galleries for additional space.

The Harris family occupied White Arches until 1873, when the family sold the house to Mr. Harris' brother-in-law, Dr. James Oliver Banks, who married a daughter of Colonel George Hampton Young of Waverley. The house remained in the Banks family until 1968.

WAVERLEY

A house that is unique in America is the plantation mansion Waverley, built in 1852 for George Hampton Young. Greek Revival motifs are incorporated into the facades (rear matches the front) with dentils on the cornice, two-story Ionic columns, and the lyre insets in front of the transom and side lights.

The hip roof rises to the dominant feature of the house—an octagonal

Waverley

Waverley — section view of cantilevered, octagonal balconies

Waverley — cupola ceiling detail

dome with sixteen windows. The ceiling of the dome—embellished with magnificent plasterwork—is fifty-two feet above the oval rotunda (Photo). The spectacular stairwell contains twin stairways that curve to the second level and a cantilevered octagonal balcony that opens into four bedrooms; a curving stairway leads to the third level–another cantilevered octagonal balcony with openings into storage rooms; a fourth stairway rises to the fourth level and another cantilevered, octagonal balcony that provides a view of the surrounding acreage (Photo).

The domed stairwell is not only beautiful, spectacular, and unique, it is also functional. In addition to providing an observatory, the sixteen windows in the cupola provide natural light for the stairwell, and, when opened, serve as a natural chimney for the hot air to rise and pass through the windows. The spacious rotunda is also ideal for balls and large-scale parties. Since Colonel Young was a wealthy landowner, a legislator, and the father of ten children who were approaching adulthood, his home was probably the scene for many social events. Mr. Reuben Davis of Aberdeen (see Sunset Hill) recalls that "Colonel Young was a man of wealth and high social standing, and his elegant home at Waverley was a centre of refined and extended hospitality."[7] Dr. William Lowndes Lipscomb wrote in his *History of Columbus, Mississippi* (published 1909), that Colonel Young's genial manners and unstinted hospitality drew a constant stream of visitors to Waverley, his country home, where "many of the most distinguished men of the state and nation were entertained."[8]

Waverley—bell lyre insets in front of red Venetian glass

The parlor, like the stairwell, contains a unique feature. Since Colonel Young's children were at marriageable ages, the parlor was designed with a wedding alcove (Photo). The room was handsomely furnished for any social occasion, with imported furniture, floral wool carpeting, a large gilded mirror over a white marble mantel, and a chandelier crafted of ormolu suspended from a plaster medallion. Fine Greek Revival millwork frames the windows that were draped with silk fabric. The splendid fabric was protected from the sun by seven linings.

Still another unique feature of Waverley can be seen in the library, the front room to the right of the entry. This room has a built-in walnut secretary with pointed arched panels and panes. Since Waverley was the hub for a sprawling plantation with many related businesses, the walnut secretary was used for the plantation post office. According to Lipscomb, Colonel Young "planted orchards, had kennels of hunting dogs, fishing boats and erected bath houses at the artesian well near the house. He built warehouses, erected a store and a large saw and grist mill and operated the ferry."[9]

The dining room is located behind the library. Like the parlor and library the room measures twenty-two by twenty-five feet and has a marble mantel, fine millwork, and a plaster ceiling medallion. To the left of the fireplace is a built-in china cabinet. The kitchen was detached and no longer exists.

Waverley—wedding alcove

The fourth room on the principal floor is a bedroom. This room, like all the others, has windows located for cross ventilation (the house contains fifty-two windows), and each room has a door that opens onto a gallery or balcony. The doors have a hand-painted grain,

Waverley — library with built in walnut secretary, marble mantel, elaborate millwork and original brass cornice

Waverley—Egyptian style millwork

porcelain door knobs, and keyhole covers. Many of the baseboards are painted to look like marble—a fad during the Greek Revival era. One of the upstairs bedrooms has Egyptian style millwork.

Waverley was built for George Hampton Young who came to Pontotoc, Mississippi, from Georgia in 1835 to attend the Indian land sales. Young, who held a law degree from Columbia College in New York and had served as a Georgia statesman, was named secretary to General Humphries who represented the government at the land sales. Young purchased land at the sale and moved his family into a house that existed on the property. In the following years he accumulated vast acreage. By 1860 his real estate was valued at $208,000 and personal assets $324,000.

J. Frazier Smith, an architect who indicated in his writings that he had access to Colonel Young's diary, attributed the design of the house to Charles I. Pond (there was an architect in St. Louis named Charles H. Pond), the mantels and marble work to Richard Miller, a Scottish craftsman from Mobile, and the ornamental plasterwork to two Irishmen from Mobile.[10] The whereabouts of this diary is not presently known.

Mrs. Young died before the mansion was completed, but she left a living memento when she planted English boxwoods in front of the house. She brought the shrubs by wagon from Georgia to enhance her first Mississippi home. When the mansion was completed, the boxwoods were set in front of the structure where they continue to flourish, despite many previous years of neglect when deer and other wild animals nibbled on the lower limbs, pruning them into their unusual shapes.

The last member of Colonel Young's family to occupy the house as a home was a bachelor son. After his death in 1913, none of the Young heirs moved into the house. The structure was left furnished for many years and members of the family would visit the homeplace occasionally. For almost fifty years the house remained unoccupied.

Between the years 1913 and 1962, people went into the house to see, to play, to write their names on the walls. While dirt daubers built their nests on some of the finest plaster walls in the state, vines grew in through the windows. In 1962, Mr. and Mrs. Robert Allen Snow, Jr., of Philadelphia, Mississippi, worked their way through the woods and found Waverley in a sad shape, but structurally sound and unaltered since construction in 1852. When Mr. Snow (who majored in history at the University of Alabama) looked through the Venetian side lights and saw the fantastic stairwell with walnut balusters outlining the gracefully curved stairs and the octagonal balconies, he knew he had to restore the work of art. Since Mrs. Snow, an antique dealer, was agreeable, arrangements were made to purchase the neglected mansion that had played such an important role in the early history of northeast Mississippi.[11]

When the news leaked out that Waverley had been purchased, curiosity seekers set out once again to visit the old house. Some of them elected to use paper torches for additional light. Because of the hazards created by the unexpected visitors, Mr. and Mrs. Snow and their three children had to move into the house sooner than they had planned. In fact, they moved in before the electricity and plumbing were installed.

Most people would have been overwhelmed by the colossal restoration project. The Snows, however, are dedicated to restoring the house to its former glory and have worked steadily toward that goal. A new roof was laid, electrical wiring installed, and bathrooms put into existing closets (a rarity in antebellum houses). The kitchen that was added to the house approximately eighty or ninety years ago is used for the kitchen-family room. Next, the immediate yard was cleared and the house painted—the original colors of course.

The original furnishings left in the house included three mirrors, (two pier mirrors in the stairwell and a large gilded mirror over the mantel in the parlor), the chandelier in the stairwell (which is suspended from a fifty-two-foot ceiling!) and the chandeliers in the parlor and library. Colonel Young used gas to light his chandeliers. Beautiful brass cornices that looked like discolored tin were found in three of the rooms. Italian marble mantels and decorative iron firebacks were still in the house, although several of the hearths had been broken, probably by treasure hunters. Only one of the red Venetian side lights had been broken. The original English carpet remains in the parlor and remnants of the original draperies.

Today (1973) the house is restored, except for the parlor, and furnished with fine antiques (i.e., Mallard and Belter pieces in the downstairs bedrooms, French and English pieces in other rooms, oriental rugs, Sevres and Meissen porcelain). The house is definitely a mansion once again and ought to be on anyone's list of historic sites that should be seen. As for the quality of the restoration, suffice it to say that Mr. and Mrs. Robert Allen Snow, Jr., were presented a National Award of Merit by the American Association for State and Local History for their restoration of Waverley.

Aberdeen

Aberdeen was founded in 1837 by a Scotsman, Robert Gordon. Gordon was a jeweler who befriended the Chickasaw Indians and then encouraged them to sell their lands to the government. In return, he was rewarded with land. He subdivided part of the property for the development of a town which he named Dundee and then later changed to Aberdeen.

The town and area were quickly settled. By 1850, the population was approximately 5,000, exceeding the size of older towns such as Natchez and Columbus. Several factors influenced this rapid development. Aberdeen had good prairie soil and was located on the "right side" of the river (next to the prairie). Thus the town became a major port on the Tombigbee River, with an economic base much greater than the population would indicate. For instance, records show that planters from Holly Springs often brought their products to Aberdeen for shipping via the Tombigbee River to Mobile.[12]

Round, fluted columns, hip roofs and exterior chimneys predominate in the designs of Aberdeen mansions. The interiors are much simpler than those of neighboring Columbus or Holly Springs. For example, none of the big houses has decorative plasterwork, interior pilasters, or marble mantels. Three of the five mansions presented in this publication have always been in the family of the builder.

SUNSET HILL

The town of Aberdeen was only ten years old when a cotton broker named William R. Cunningham built his "Greek Temple" known today as Sunset Hill. The T-shaped structure appears rather masculine, with its facade free of decoration except for the eight substantial Doric

Sunset Hill

columns that extend across the front and partially around two sides. The low-pitched hip roof and the deep entablature above the columns and the double doors emphasize the horizontal lines of the house.

In addition to the typical eight-room, central hallway Greek Revival plan, there are rooms on each side that give the house its T-shape. Also, the house previously had an ell attached to the right for a service wing. For convenience, a small service stair leads from the right side of the house into a cross hall upstairs. The service stair is supplementary to the main stairway in the center hall.

The beauty of the house is enhanced by its location some distance from the street. A wide brick walkway, bordered with boxwoods, leads to the double-door entry. Ancient magnolia trees grace the lawn.

Many people refer to the house as the Reuben Davis House in reference to its well-known occupant from 1867-1890 who had studied medicine, was a successful lawyer, a soldier, a judge, an author (*Recollections of Mississippi and Mississippians*), and a legislator.

THE MAGNOLIAS

Across the street from the Davis house is The Magnolias. Massive magnolia trees line the wide brick walk that leads to a spacious portico with the entry emphasized by paired columns, double doors, and stained-glass side lights. A simple, paneled parapet crowns the front roof line.

The house was built for Dr. William Alfred Sykes, who came with his two brothers to Aberdeen from Virginia. They became large land-

The Magnolias — unusual tri-level stairway

The Magnolias

The Magnolias — well house

The Magnolias — kitchen

The Magnolias — second story view of stairway

owners and wealthy planters. In 1850, Dr. Sykes built this three-story town house that has always been occupied by his descendants. The house still contains some original furnishings.

The Magnolias has a tri-level stairwell that is especially noteworthy. Steps rise from both the front and rear of the center hallway along the right wall, meet in the center, cross over to the opposite side of the hall, and then separate once again before continuing the ascent to the second level (Photo A: Taken from rear of hallway. Photo B: Taken from upper level). Crystal banquet lamps adorn each newel post. These lamps came from the First Methodist Church, which was built in 1859.

The doorway underneath the stairs leads to another stairway, which gave access to the dining room and storage rooms in the basement. The dining room was in the basement for easy access from the detached kitchen (Photos: Kitchen and Well House).

Double parlors are located to the left of the entry. The parlors were the setting for a tableau wedding once with the wedding party in the rear parlor and the guests in the front parlor. When the sliding doors that separate the two rooms were opened, the wedding ceremony began.

OLD HOMESTEAD

Dr. Augustus Sykes was the youngest of the three Sykes brothers who migrated to Aberdeen from Virginia. According to Reuben Davis, Dr. Sykes ". . . possessed the same general characteristics (as his brothers), but was perhaps of a more ardent and active temperament, and of a more social nature. He was possessed of large fortune, which he lived to enjoy to an advanced age."

In 1852 Dr. Sykes lived in Sunset Hill while his Old Homestead was being constructed. The two-story house with an exposed basement has twin porticoes with the main entrance facing Commerce Street. Originally the portico roofs were ornamented with decorative woodwork.

The Old Homestead has remained in the Sykes family and contains several pieces of original furnishings. The carriage house is contemporary with the house and was executed in the picturesque Gothic style (Photo).

Old Homestead

Old Homestead — carriage house

137

ST. JOHN'S EPISCOPAL CHURCH

St. John's Episcopal Church is significant because of its first rector and its design. The rector was Joseph Holt Ingraham who was born in Portland, Maine. Ingraham came to the Natchez area where he became a teacher of languages at the Jefferson College. He married Miss Mary Brookes, the daughter of a local planter, and began to write descriptions of his travels in Mississippi and Louisiana. The descriptions were published in 1835 in two volumes under the title *The South-west.* Ingraham became a prolific writer of romantic fiction, producing as many as twenty novels in one year. These novels seemed to have made up in money what they lacked in quality. Henry Wadsworth Longfellow wrote to a friend regarding Professor Ingraham: "I think he may say that he writes the worst novels ever written by anybody. But they sell; he gets twelve hundred dollars for them."[14]

Ingraham's way of life changed in 1847 when he became interested in the church and was confirmed as a communicant in the Protestant Episcopal Church. This change did not go unnoticed. The following excerpt appeared in the *Knickerbocker:*

> Professor Ingraham, who has within the last few years written more immoral works than any other of the many penny-a-line scribblers to whom the "cheap and nasty" school of ephemeral productions have given birth, has taken to the church for a "living!"

Ingraham's first position after his confirmation was headmaster at a religious school for young women in Nashville, Tennessee. He changed positions several times before he arrived in Aberdeen on April 2, 1851, to serve as the leader for St. John's Mission. The cornerstone for St. John's Episcopal Church was laid in October of that same year. Ingraham wrote to Bishop Green in May, 1853, regarding the church:

> . . . the whole cost is nearly $7,000.00 . . . In order to complete the church and let every dollar go towards the building I have received no regular salary and have taught for my maintenance . . . There being no church architect here who had any knowledge of Gothic construction, I was compelled not only to be the draughtsman but contractor and architect of the building, erecting it with the aid of two young men and nine slaves.[15]

In 1853 Ingraham resigned from his position at Aberdeen and was dismissed in January 1854. He became the rector for a new church in Mobile, Alabama. While serving at St. John's in Mobile, Ingraham wrote his first biblical novel *The Prince of the House of David* (which brought him fame). Ingraham resigned from his Mobile position in 1856 because of the inadequate salary. He moved to Riverside, Tennessee, to become headmaster for an Episcopal School. Records indicate his stay in Tennessee was a short one since he was back in Natchez in 1857. In 1858 he was officially transferred from the Diocese of Tennessee to the Diocese of Mississippi. At this time he went to Holly Springs to become the rector for Christ Church and to supervise St. Thomas Hall, a school for boys. The church at Holly Springs was a new building that was consecrated on October 6, 1858 (see Holly Springs section). In addition to his dual role at Holly Springs, Ingraham also found time to write two more biblical novels, *The Pillar of Fire* and *The*

St. John's Episcopal Church

Throne of David, and to publish a series of letters, *The Sunny South*. His plans for a fourth religious novel were never realized since Ingraham was shot in the vestry room of Christ Church. Some people attribute his death to suicide; others claim it was accidental. He died eight days after the shot and was buried in Holly Springs. His novels continued to sell and a new edition of *The Prince of the House of David* appeared in London as late as 1939.[16] St. John's Episcopal Church in Aberdeen is a beautiful landmark that is a tribute to Joseph Holt Ingraham's versatility. The Gothic structure has beautiful stained glass windows and a slave gallery. Since the building is located on the main thoroughfare it can be appreciated by the many people who pass it each day.

Two of the more decorative houses in Aberdeen are Holliday Haven (1850) and the Masonic Temple (1856), both located on Meridian Street. Holliday Haven, the earlier house, features paired Doric columns, while the Masonic Temple has the more ornate Ionic columns. Paired columns were used frequently in Oxford and occasionally in Columbus. However, they were probably used most effectively in these two Aberdeen mansions.

The degree of paneling on the facade of these two houses is much greater than on other houses in Mississippi. Paired pilasters repeat the twin motif, while the ceilings are coffered.

HOLLIDAY HAVEN

Holliday Haven was built for John Holliday, a planter who came to this area from North Carolina. The house was originally two stories in the front and only one story in the rear. After an abundant cotton crop around the year 1922, the back part of the house was enlarged to become two stories high, and the stairway was altered.

The spacious house with supporting buildings (smokehouse, storage house, greenhouse) is located on a six-acre lot that was once enclosed by an iron fence. The house still remains in the family of the builder.

MASONIC TEMPLE

The imposing Masonic Temple, known in earlier years as the Adams, or French House was built by John Cox for his daughter Mrs. Robert S. Adams whose husband was a businessman in Aberdeen. After Mr. Adams died in 1872, Mrs. Adams married Dr. Andrew French. The Masons bought the house in the 1940s and changed the roof line from flat to hip.[17] Interior alterations were made to make the building more suitable to the needs of the organization. The facade, with its symmetry incorporating paired columns, paired pilasters, paired windows, and three balconies with decorative iron rails, is still intact for present generations to enjoy.

Holliday Haven

Masonic Temple

DUNLEE

Aberdeen has many fine antebellum cottages. Dunlee was selected to be representative of this group with its simple pediment supported by two pairs of square columns, double doors with side and transom lights, and a center hallway. These features are typical of cottages in Aberdeen, Oxford, and Holly Springs.

Dunlee was built in 1853 by Dr. William A. Dunklin, a South Carolinian who was a planter and merchant. The double-hung, twelve-over-twelve front windows of Dunlee are especially attractive. The house has a side porch located to the left of the library. Entry onto the porch is through the window. Millwork in the house is Greek Revival in style. The house is surrounded by a brick walkway, while magnolias accent the entry.

Dunlee

KANSAS CITY, MOBILE, AND BIRMINGHAM RAILWAY STATION

The design for the Kansas City, Mobile, and Birmingham Railway Station was executed by the famous architects Daniel H. Burnham and John W. Root of Chicago.[18] The station was designed in 1888 and demolished in 1972.

Burnham and Root built many of the landmarks in Chicago. Burnham was chief of construction for the Chicago Fair and president of the American Institute of Architects; he developed plans for improving the cities Washington, D.C.; Cleveland, Ohio; San Francisco, California; Chicago, Illinois; and two cities in the Philippine Islands.

FIRST METHODIST CHURCH

The present building was constructed in 1912 on the site of the old church. Architect R. H. Hunt of Chattanooga, Tennessee drew the plans and Mr. Terry McClannahan of Columbus was the contractor.[19] The edifice is rectangular but the sanctuary is octagonal. Two walls are dominated by stained glass murals that have been attributed to Louis

Kansas City, Mobile, and Birmingham Railway Station — destroyed. An early design of the famous architectural firm Burnham and Root of Chicago.

First Methodist Church

Comfort Tiffany. The chandeliers suspended from brass chains are also attributed to the famous New York artist. In 1968 the church was refurbished to complement the brilliant colors of the windows and bullet-proof glass was installed over the glass.

LENOIR PLANTATION HOUSE

Ten miles north of West Point is the Lenoir Plantation House which was built in 1847 as a story-and-a-half structure for Mr. William Thomas Lenoir, a planter from South Carolina. The house was enlarged and the stairway changed in 1910. The house has always been occupied by Lenoirs with the present owner being Mr. and Mrs. Whitman H. Lenoir. Some of the original furnishings are still used at the plantation house.

Lenoir Plantation House

Pontotoc

LOCHINVAR

A Scotsman named Robert Gordon was responsible for the construction of the lovely mansion named Lochinvar that is located on a ridge near Pontotoc. Gordon was a land speculator who encouraged the Chickasaw Indians to cede their property to the United States government in 1832. He was rewarded with land which he divided into lots to form a town — Aberdeen. Because of the good soil and the location on the Tombigbee River ,the town was settled quickly and by 1850 had a population of nearly 5,000.

Robert Gordon, however, chose to live in Pontotoc where the government land office was established in 1836. According to the 1840 census, he had forty slaves with fifteen engaged in agriculture. By 1860 Gordon had accumulated real estate valued at $200,000 and $180,000 in personal property.

The Scotsman who had married a Virginian, Mary Elizabeth Walton, purchased the site for his mansion in 1836. He proceeded to build one of the largest houses in Mississippi. Lochinvar has classic details with the simple pediment supported by four modified Tuscan columns. The doorway ensemble is especially attractive with Ionic columns *in antis.* Rectangular transom lights span the double door while pilasters and

Lochinvar

Lochinvar — door detail

side lights frame the sides. The motif employed for the rail of the second floor gallery depicts reeds tied to form an interesting pattern.

The architectural elements of the entrance hall are especially fine. An arch divides the length of the hall and appears to be supported by paired pilasters. The arch and pilasters are paneled. A spectacular stairway sweeps from right to left at the rear of the hall and spirals up for three levels. A second stairway, located in the attic, provided access to the octagonal cupola (now gone).

The house contains eight principal rooms—each measuring twenty-two feet square. To the left of the entry are double parlors that can be separated by folding doors. The fine quality millwork features the Greek crossettes. The simple wooden mantels project at five intervals. French doors open onto an eighteen-foot-wide gallery that spans the side of the parlors and the rear of the house.

An unusual feature of the floor plan is a service staircase that rises from the dining room to the bedroom apartments. The house has a spacious attic lighted by two windows at each end of the gabled roof. The sturdy construction of Lochinvar can be noted in the basement (Photo).

The rural setting greatly enhances the beauty of the house. A narrow, curving road meanders across the acres to the stately classic mansion that is landscaped with cedars and English boxwoods as old as the house.

Colonel James Gordon inherited the property after his father's death in 1867. In 1900 J. D. Fontaine, a Pontotoc attorney became the owner of Lochinvar; in 1926 his son assumed ownership. Dr. Forrest Tutor, present owner, purchased the house in 1966.

Lochinvar — heavy beams

Oxford

The town of Oxford developed on land that was ceded to the United States by the Chickasaw Indian Nation in 1832. The town was incorporated in 1837, with the major businesses located around the courthouse square. A fire in 1864, started by A. J. "Whiskey" Smith in retaliation for the Fort Pillow massacre, destroyed the courthouse, thirty-four stores and two businesses, two hotels, and five fine dwellings.[20]

There is much sameness in the design of the early Oxford houses. They are two-story wood structures fronted with tall, square columns that are often paired. The reverse-L floor plan was popular. Owing to the simplicity and lack of architectural orders, this type of house is frequently referred to as "Mississippi Planter Style." However, the houses of this type in Oxford were not built by planters. A doctor had the Isom Place built; Circuit Judge James M. Howry had the Howry-Wright-Purser House constructed; Colonel Robert Shegog, a trader from Virginia, built Rowan Oak; Shadowlawn was the home of merchant W. S. Neilson; and Cedar Oaks was erected by William Turner, a builder.

ISOM PLACE

Isom Place, one of the oldest houses in Oxford, encompasses a log cabin. Inside it is easy to distinguish the cabin since its ceiling height is approximately nine feet compared to thirteen feet, nine inches in the newer areas.

Isom Place was the home of one of Oxford's first settlers, Thomas Dudley Isom, who came to the Oxford area from Tennessee around 1835 to trade with the Indians. He later became a pioneer doctor.

HOWRY-WRIGHT-PURSER HOUSE

The Howry-Wright-Purser House was constructed for Judge James M. Howry who came to Oxford in 1836 from Tennessee. Judge Howry was one of the first trustees for the University of Mississippi. In 1884, Charles B. Howry inherited the house. He had his father's law office, which was located in the yard, attached to the left side of the house. Charles Howry, who was the first law student to graduate from the University of Mississippi law school after the Civil War, served as a judge in the United States Court of Claims and as the assistant attorney general under Grover Cleveland. When he left Oxford for Washington, he sold the house to Dr. Patrick H. Wright, a dentist. Mrs. Wright designed a Victorian exterior for her house. When Mrs. Frank Purser, daughter of Dr. Wright, bought the house, she had the exterior restored to the original order. New columns replaced the old ones that had been burned. The decorative iron balustrade was brought from Mr. Purser's home in Tuscaloosa, Alabama.[21]

Isom Place

Howry-Wright, Purser House

Rowan Oak — William Faulkner's house, designated as a National Historic Landmark

ROWAN OAK

Rowan Oak was built for Colonel Robert Shegog. Most people, however, associate the house with the man who named it—William Faulkner, Nobel Prize-winning author. Faulkner acquired the house in 1930. He added the balustrade on each side of the house and built a room behind the library (west side) for his office. The house was easily enlarged since the original floorplan was a reverse-L.

The room that Faulkner added is probably the most famous in Oxford. People travel from all over the United States and foreign countries to visit the room where Faulkner wrote many of his famous novels. Visitors usually notice the walls of the office immediately. They have been described by many distinguished scholars as the most literary walls in the world. The writing here is an outline of the plot for the novel *A Fable*.

The wooded and secluded setting for the house afforded the writer some privacy. The entry to the site is picturesque, with the narrow, winding driveway lined by iris and ancient cedar trees. Tall cedars also outline the wide brick walkway that leads to the house. Years

Rowan Oak — study. Faulkner outlined the plot for his novel *The Fable* on the walls.

ago the grounds were landscaped with formal gardens, but the garden to the south, encircled by cedars has not been maintained in its original formal state because, according to some of the members of the family, Faulkner wished it to have a natural or primitive appearance. In the secluded garden in the rear, one sees Faulkner's formal garden with its wisteria vines, pear trees, pecans, and a scuppernong arbor (reminiscent of the one Colonel Sutpen and Wash Jones must have sat under on a late August afternoon recollecting Colonel Sutpen's exploits in the war that the South had lost, by now already assuming legendary qualities).

A two-room brick building contemporary with the house is located in the rear yard. Faulkner used the west room for storage and the east one for a smokehouse. Also behind the house is a log stable for which local tradition says Faulkner himself did the rechinking.

The house and grounds adjoin the University of Mississippi campus and are maintained by the University for memorial and educational purposes.

Rowan Oak — log barn rechinked by William Faulkner

SHADOWLAWN

Shadowlawn, built for merchant W. S. Neilson, founder of Neilson Department Store, is striking because of its size and the twin entrances. The original reverse-L floorplan was similar to that of Rowan Oak. The house has been enlarged in recent years and improved by changing the straight, narrow stairway to one that is more accessible. An attractive patio at Shadowlawn is made of wedge-shaped bricks from the columns of the first courthouse which was burned.

CEDAR OAKS

Cedar Oaks, built in 1859, was the home of William Turner who probably designed and built Shadowlawn, the Thompson-Chandler House, Cedar Oaks, and other similar houses in Oxford. However,

Shadowlawn

Cedar Oaks — cut in half to facilitate moving the large structure to its present site. Note the seam in pediment.

Cedar Oaks is more decorative than the other houses—with brackets under the eaves, a fanciful balcony balustrade, and a belvedere on the roof (now gone). The treatment of the doorway and the interior woodwork indicates a Greek Revival influence.

Oxford is fortunate still to have Cedar Oaks, since two serious threats of destruction were made. The first occurred in 1864 when downtown Oxford was burned by Union forces under the direction of General A. J. Smith. Cedar Oaks was located just one block away from the courthouse and the thirty-four businesses that were destroyed.

The second threat arrived almost one century later when space was needed for a new motor hotel. The lot that Cedar Oaks occupied appeared to be the ideal spot. Owners of the house offered the building to the city of Oxford and to the University of Mississippi, but neither party was interested. Then, a group of club women, led by Mrs. Bryan Tate, formed Oxford-Lafayette Historic Homes, Inc., and set out to save the house. Land was donated, money raised, and a mortgage obtained. Next, the ladies had to get Cedar Oaks to its destination two and one-half miles away! To accomplish this feat the house was cut in half, and 114 wires in the town were lowered, raised, or spliced (involving three utility companies) to allow the big house to pass through Oxford's streets. In addition, a road eight-tenths of a mile long had to be constructed. The ladies got the job done on August 29, 1963. Within six months the house was put back together, painted, and furnished. Futhermore, the club women started an annual pilgrimage that year and were delighted to have Cedar Oaks as the headquarters.

L. Q. C. LAMAR HOUSE

A small cottage probably built by Mr. Alford Barger around 1856 was later occupied by the outstanding statesman L. Q. C. Lamar. Lamar, a lawyer and a congressman, was named by President Grover

L. Q. C. Lamar House — facade altered

Cleveland to be secretary of the interior and, in 1887, was appointed to the United States Supreme Court.

The Oxford house was purchased on June 18, 1868, by Lamar's wife. The property joined her father's land. Her father, Augustus B. Longstreet, was a lawyer, writer, Methodist clergyman, and educator. He was the second president of the University of Mississippi.

The original floor plan for the simple house contained four rooms, measuring twenty feet square, and a hallway. Timbers are held together with wooden pegs. The porch has been altered.

LYCEUM BUILDING

The Lyceum Building with its beautifully executed Ionic capitals is probably one of the most photographed buildings in the state. The classic structure has served as the hub for the University of Mississippi campus since its doors were opened for eighty students in 1848.

The building was designed by architect William Nichols who had previously designed buildings for the University of Alabama, the Mississippi capitol building and the Mississippi governor's mansion. The design that Nichols submitted to the Board of Trustees was adapted

Lyceum Building

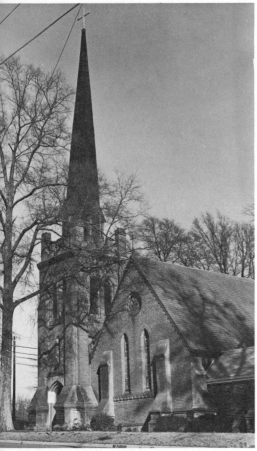

St. Peter's Episcopal Church

by dispensing with the foundation story and adding another story. The three-story structure provided two classrooms, a chemical-theater for lectures, and a large laboratory on the first floor; additional classrooms and a museum for shells, geological specimens, and other artifacts were located on the second floor; the library and more classrooms were situated on the third level. The lumber for the building was provided by David Craig, the brick work by O. B. and J. W. Crary, carpenter work by Daniel Graywon and Burrage Heathman, gutter work by James Smith and blacksmith work by William Floyd.

While the Lyceum Building was being constructed, Mr. Nichols occupied a house on the University property so that he would be convenient for superintending the work.[22] The minutes of the Board of Trustees for the University of Mississippi indicate that Nichols' duties included the protection and preservation of the lumber and other materials about the University from depredation, and also the prevention of any person from trespassing upon the University section by cutting timber.[23]

The initial building accommodated the University of Mississippi enrollment until 1858 when the building was lengthened by about one third. The building was expanded again in 1903 by adding two wings to the tall structure. The west portico with columns was added in 1923, thus making the building symmetrical. The Lyceum Building is presently used for administrative offices.

ST. PETER'S EPISCOPAL CHURCH

A note on the back of the church deed attributes the design of this Episcopal church (1855) to Richard Upjohn, a famed English architect. Although the spire was a part of the original plan, it was not constructed until 1893 — a gift of Mrs. Alexander Pegues.

AMMADELLE

Oxford's Ammadelle is one of the finest Italianate houses in the South. The design of the substantial, solid-brick structure is a sharp contrast to the other Oxford houses. Its asymmetrical facade offers "elegant variety" — a term Andrew Downing liked to use in reference to Italianate buildings. Downing, a landscape architect and architectural critic of the mid-nineteenth century, considered the Italianate style to be the preferred style for country residences:

> It addresses itself more to the feelings and the senses, and less to the reason or judgment, than the Grecian style, and it is also capable of a variety of expression quite unknown to the architecture of the five orders. Hence, we think it far better suited to symbolize the variety of a refined culture and accomplishment which belongs to modern civilization than almost any other style.[24]

The assemblage of the arched windows with canopies, the overhanging eaves with brackets, the balconies with decorative balustrades, the bay windows with shaped bricks at the corners, and the arcades with numerous arches, into an Italian villa is credited to Calvert Vaux, an English architect who was brought to this country by Andrew Downing in 1850. Vaux is probably most widely known for his design (with partner Frederick Law Olmstead) for Central Park in New York and for his book *Villas and Cottages*. The exterior of Ammadelle cor-

Ammadelle

responds very closely with the plan that was published in *Harper's New Monthly Magazine* in November 1855 in the article by Vaux, "Hints for Country House Builders."[25] The plan also appeared as Design No. 27, An Irregular Villa Without Wing in the first edition of Vaux's book *Villas and Cottages* published in 1857.[26] The original plans for Ammadelle with Vaux's name printed on the lower right corner are framed and are on display in the library of the villa. Vaux published his fee schedule in his book:

> 2½ per ct for plans and specifications
> 1   per ct for detail drawings
> 1½ per ct Superintendence
> ——
> 5   per ct usual commission of architects

Ammadelle was built for Thomas Pegues who was a landowner, a University of Mississippi trustee, and director of the Mississippi Central Railroad. The house has an irregular floor plan which is typical of Italianate structures. Entry is through arched double doors into a foyer. The staircase is located in the hall behind the foyer and is separated from the foyer by an arched doorway with sliding doors.

Ammadelle — elevation prepared by English architect Calvert Vaux

Ammadelle — millwork detail

The dining room is to the left of the entrance hall and it, too, is separated from the foyer by sliding doors with arched-shaped millwork. The dining room appears very light and spacious with its fourteen-foot ceiling, two floor-length windows on the front of the house and another floor-length window on the side that opens into a five-bay window plant conservatory. The conservatory is especially attractive with the floor-length windows finished at the top with rounded arches. The butler's pantry and kitchen (Photo) are behind and to the left of the dining room. These rooms are a part of the main house and not detached as was the custom for Greek Revival buildings.

Double parlors, sometimes referred to as the drawing room and the morning room, are located to the right of the entrance hall. The parlors have both bay windows and double-hung windows with panes that measure 32½ inches by 22 inches. The windows are floor length to open onto balconies, porches, arcades — assets for houses located in warm climates.

A small library with built in bookcases is located to the right of the back parlor. The room has an attractive wood mantel (Photo) and an exterior door that opens onto a loggia.

The downstairs floor plan also contains a back stairway and a boudoir that are located to the left of the main stair well. Downing recommended that the boudoir "... be very tastefully and prettily fitted up, and used

Ammadelle — mantel in library

Ammadelle — fireplace in attached kitchen

by the lady of the house as a morning room for receiving social calls; or, if preferred, it would serve admirably as a dressing room. . . ."[27] Four sleeping apartments are located upstairs.

Ammadelle is truly a fine example of Italianate architecture with its asymmetrical facade ornamented with rounded arches of various sizes. The brackets, clustered chimneys, arcades, porches, balconies, and canopies all add to the "elegant variety" of the Italian villa.

The design of the spacious lawn is appropriate for the house with magnolias and other native plants spaced irregularly while ancient boxwoods line the circular drive. The entourage is as "pretty as a picture." Perhaps that explains why Ammadelle was selected for scenes in *Home from the Hills,* a movie starring Robert Mitchum.

FIDDLER'S FOLLY

According to local tradition, Fiddler's Folly is a prefabricated house (1878) that was precut and shipped to Oxford to speed up construction. Judge Charles Howry had the house constructed for his wife who was ill.

Italianate features predominate in the design of the house with the arched, paired and bay windows, decorative brackets under the eaves and paired columns. The wood is scored to look like stone.

Fiddler's Folly

Holly Springs

Until the early 1830s, the Chickasaw Indians occupied the "high and dry" hilly area of North Mississippi that was naturally landscaped with holly trees and free-flowing springs. After the Chickasaw cession, people came from many directions to take advantage of the rich farm lands. By 1836 counties had been designated and a town square was taking shape in Holly Springs, the seat of Marshall County.

Owing to the mass migration of people to the area to buy and sell land, the region also became a fertile operation site for lawyers. By March, 1838, the circuit court in Holly Springs had 1,200 cases on the docket. Records show that in 1840 approximately forty lawyers had established offices in Holly Springs.[28]

Many of the early settlers of Holly Springs were learned men who wanted comfortable homes, good schools and churches, as well as cultural activities for their families. Consequently, before Holly Springs was incorporated as a town, the local people met to plan an academy. The following year, money was raised to build a brick building to house the University of Holly Springs. The building is now used as a private home (Photo). This was the first time such an ambitious title had been used for an educational institution in the state. Records indicate that in 1860 the city of Holly Springs spent more on education than the rest of the state combined, except for the University of Mississippi.

Holly Springs has been the home town of thirteen generals, one admiral, six United States senators, ten United States congressmen, eighteen judges, seven authors, and two well-known painters. This record is especially impressive for a town whose population numbered approximately 3,000 in 1860 and 8,000 in 1970.

University of Holly Springs

LAND OFFICE

One of the first buildings constructed in Holly Springs was a land office to house the many governmental land transactions. The small brick office still exists on the corner of Memphis Street and Gholson Avenue, though it originally faced west instead of south. The building is important in the history of Holly Springs, not only because of its early function, but also because it was the first brick structure in the city, and in addition, the yellow fever epidemic in Holly Springs began here in 1878.

Land Office

FIRST PRESBYTERIAN CHURCH

Holly Springs has many historic churches, with the First Presbyterian Church being one of the largest structures. In 1860 construction was started on the present building, which is located on the same site as three previous Presbyterian churches. Only the walls, roof, and basement were completed before the War Between the States commenced. The large building provided shelter for horses during the conflict. The church was completed in 1869 after the Reverend H. H.

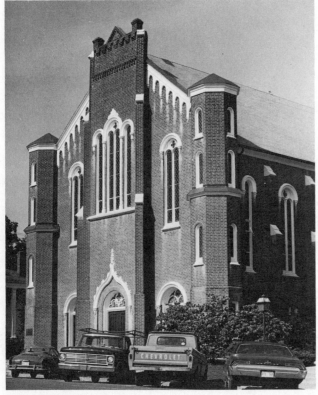
First Presbyterian Church

Many of the steps in Holly Springs are made of rounded bricks.

Paine traveled to northern and midwestern states to raise money to restore and complete the construction.

The church, like many buildings in Holly Springs, was constructed of brick since the clay in the area is especially good for brick. Numerous houses have solid-brick construction with the interior walls measuring eighteen or more inches in thickness. The houses are not on piers; instead, each wall goes completely to the ground. This gives a sturdy foundation, but certainly complicated matters when later owners installed electricity, plumbing, central heating, and air-conditioning.

A rounded brick was made for use as steps. Examples of this type brick can be seen in various parts of the town. The ones photographed are located to the left of the Presbyterian Church.

CHRIST CHURCH

The Episcopal Church is a good example of Gothic architecture that contains colorful stained glass windows and fine wood detail. The building was consecrated on October 6, 1858. The rector at this time was Joseph Holt Ingraham who had formerly been the rector for Aberdeen's St. John's Episcopal Church — a church he designed and constructed (see Aberdeen section).

HOLLY SPRINGS DEPOT

A pleasant surprise among the architectural edifices of Holly Springs is a massive building that looks like a French Renaissance castle. Upon closer examination, however, one will note that railroad tracks front the building. This structure was built as an elegant depot-hotel with twenty bedrooms, a dining room-ballroom that would accommodate 125 people, and many service rooms.

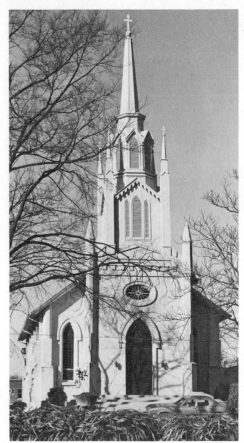
Christ Church

The Depot

The northwest wing of the building was constructed in the 1850s by the Mississippi Central Railroad. The building was enlarged by the Illinois Central Railroad with the addition of the front, or east, section. A roofer dated a front rafter "3-21-1886."

The steep roof design, replete with dormers, towers, and finials, is picturesque. The design was adapted for function by adding a wide, wooden canopy to shade the railway customers from the weather. The elements of the building design are harmonious, with the brick detail and other features being subordinate to the major design feature — the roof.

The hotel-depot is now a private home but has been altered very little architecturally. The major change involved joining the northwest and southwest wings via a roof and a wall to form a courtyard.

BANK OF HOLLY SPRINGS

The Bank of Holly Springs opened for business on February 1, 1869, in the building that it still occupies (Photo: Last Building on Right). The bank is the oldest state bank and the second oldest of all banks in Mississippi. The side stairway leads to lawyers' offices. The oldest buildings in downtown Holly Springs are on the south side of the square.

Bank of Holly Springs

The name Harris Gholson is immediately associated with the Bank of Holly Springs by local residents and members of banking circles. Harris became the bank's bookkeeper in 1914 and worked his way up to become president in 1946. In 1971, at the age of eighty-three, he was still associated with the bank and enjoyed relating the story of a deposit of $1,000 being made by a Mississippi Negro senator, Hiram Revels, in 1870. After Senator Revels' term in Washington, he moved to California, where he died without known heirs. Thus the $1,000 remained unclaimed in the bank. In 1964, Gholson heard a speech at the Republican national convention by a Mississippi delegate who stated he was the son-in-law of Senator Hiram Revels. From this clue, heirs of the senator were found and given the money. Gholson was happy that the money was a demand deposit instead of a time deposit!

Some of the older houses in Holly Springs are Tallaloosa, Feather-ston Place, Tuckahoe, Mosswood, Crump, White Pillars, Herndon, and Latoka.

TALLALOOSA

Tallaloosa is a log house of the dog-trot type which was restored by members of the Walter family. The house has two main rooms joined by a breezeway that has been enclosed. (Photo: Behind the house is a detached kitchen. Note log construction.)

Tallaloosa — log, dog-trot

Tallaloosa — detail of log construction

Featherston Place

Tuckahoe

Mosswood

Crump Place

FEATHERSTON PLACE AND TUCKAHOE

Since Featherston Place and Tuckahoe are located on adjacent lots and have similar architectural and landscape features, they are presented together here. The houses are referred to locally as the English raised basement type. The parlor and bedrooms are located on the first floor, while the dining room, kitchen and storage rooms are in the basement. The basement of each house is exposed and outlined by a brick walk and an elevated decorative iron fence. This arrangement is suggestive of a moat.

Featherston Place was built by Alexander McEwen, a merchant from Tennessee. General Thomas Polk, brother of the famous "fighting Bishop" General Leonidas Polk and a cousin of President James Knox Polk, built Tuckahoe. Both houses feature a fanlighted entrance. The houses were restored in 1917 by architect Theodore C. Link and beautifully landscaped by a Mr. Kiern, both of St. Louis, for Oscar Johnson. Johnson, who owned Walter Place, bought and restored several houses that joined his property.

MOSSWOOD

Mosswood also has an exposed basement that originally housed the kitchen. The house was constructed by Adrian Mayer, a lawyer from South Carolina. It has been renovated by Fredonia Johnson Moss, granddaughter of Holly Springs leader Harvey Walter, who constructed Walter Place. The house contains many oriental furnishings that were inherited by Mrs. Moss from her late aunt, Dr. Ann Walter Fearn, who was a surgeon in Shanghai, China.

CRUMP PLACE

Crump Place was built by Samuel McCorkle, who was the first land commissioner for the Holly Springs area. McCorkle came from Virginia and became the first banker in the county. The gallery entry is unusual with recessed steps.

WHITE PILLARS

Thomas Falconer, who was editor of the newspaper *South,* had White Pillars constructed. His son, Kinlock, was a state leader who served as secretary of state. Both father and son died during the yellow fever

White Pillars

epidemic. The octagonal columns and decorative balcony are the major design features for this stately house.

HERNDON

Herndon, lacking a portico and being located close to the street, is not a typical southern home. Its builder was Louis Thompson of Massachusetts who built the house like those he saw back home. Before the house was enlarged by adding rooms to the left side, the floor plan was very similar to New England town houses with an asymmetrical entry into a hallway. The parlor and dining room were on the first floor, the bedroom upstairs, and the kitchen in the basement. The house is devoid of decoration except for the shaped lintels and the decorative iron ventilators.

The size of the house was increased by attaching rooms to the left and building a detached kitchen, which was five steps lower than the main building. Today the kitchen has been raised and attached.

Herndon is probably the oldest two-story brick house in Holly Springs.

Herndon

LATOKA

Latoka was named for an Indian princess who lived in this area before Holly Springs was founded as a town. Mrs. Claude Smith, present owner, said "the house is too small to be named for a Queen." The size of the house is one of its outstanding features. Being located in a town where large houses are plentiful, Latoka appears to be a miniature replica.

The well-proportioned two-bedroom brick house with classic lines was built by W. S. Randolph. The interior is finished with a simple plaster mold and cast-iron mantels.

Latoka — named for an Indian princess

WALTHALL-FREEMAN

This small cottage, decorated with Italianate arches and slender colonettes, was the childhood home of Confederate General Edward

Walthall-Freeman

Cary Marshall, a lawyer who served as a United States senator from 1885 to 1898. Kate Freeman Clark, grandniece of Senator Walthall, inherited the house in later years. Miss Clark studied art in New York City and became a prolific painter who chose not to sell her paintings. When she died, she willed to the city of Holly Springs the Walthall-Freeman House, all of her paintings (over one thousand), and money to construct a gallery for her paintings.

Most of the larger houses in Holly Springs were built between the years 1850 and 1860. This was an especially prosperous decade for Holly Springs as more cotton was produced in Marshall County during this period than in any other county in Mississippi. Since money was plentiful, the houses had many "little extras" in the way of decoration. For example, the Greek Revival houses appear to have been dressed with decorative castiron lintels, grillwork for the balconies, and iron fences — many of which were made at the local foundry. The interiors featured curved stairways, stained glass side lights, plaster medallions and cornices, and marble mantels.

During the latter part of the decade, some builders chose to build Gothic structures rather than decorated Greek Revival. During the transitional period from Greek to Gothic Harvey Walter decided to use both classic and romantic characteristics for his mansion, which he accomplished by combining a Greek Revival portico with Gothic towers. Another transitional house was The Magnolias which shows Gothic tendencies with its pointed-arch window and door. Two houses that are definitely Gothic are Cedarhurst and Airliewood.

Many of the fine mansions are located on Salem Street, a fact that has led to the epithet "Silk-Stocking Avenue" in later years. Notice in the pictorial presentation how the houses became more decorative as the decade progressed.

FORT DANIEL

One of the first "big houses" constructed in Holly Springs is the Fort Daniel house built around 1850. The Greek Revival influence is

Fort Daniel — ornate gate

Fort Daniel

seen in the two-story columns that front three sides of the structure. The house construction is unusual in that the brick walls are insulated with charcoal. This feature was discovered when the house was wired for electricity. The house is one of a few houses in Mississippi that has remained in the family of the builder since construction.

The decorative iron fence and gate contrast sharply with the house that is devoid of ornamentation (Photo).

MAGNOLIAS

The design of Magnolias is a good blending of Greek and Gothic Revival features with the formal floor plan representing the Classic style, while the broken roof line, pointed-arch windows with diamond-shaped panes, and the decorative iron grillwork contribute to the picturesque Gothic look.

The house was built around the mid-nineteenth century by William F. Mason, who was originally from Baltimore. Mr. Mason was treasurer of the Illinois Central Railroad.

The exterior of this substantial house is of stuccoed brick. The center hallway contains an attractive curved stairway. The pointed-arch design was carried out in the landscaping with the bricks being laid in an arched pattern. Magnificent magnolia trees on the property prompted the name for the house.

Magnolias

Three houses with similar features were built about the same time on Salem Avenue. Maxland, Oakleigh, and Montrose are similar in that they are two-story brick structures with four grooved columns topped with capitals embellished with acanthus leaves (Photo: detail of Maxland capital). The design of the capital is similar to those on the octagon tower in Athens, Greece. Each house has a balcony with a decorative iron balustrade. The windows are trimmed with ornate lintels and wooden shutters.

Maxland — detail of capital

MAXLAND

Maxland differs from Oakleigh and Montrose in that the pediment was omitted and the house was L-shaped. It is believed that the house

Maxland

was constructed by G. A. Palm, a German, for Joel Wynne, a cotton buyer. When Mr. Wynne left Holly Springs to go to Arkansas (Wynne, Arkansas, is named for him), Mr. Palm bought Maxland.

OAKLEIGH

One of the finer mansions in Holly Springs and Mississippi is Oakleigh, built by Judge J. W. Clapp and now the home of Mr. and Mrs. Glenn Fant. The two-story classic structure is ornamented with a fanlighted pediment; a cornice emphasized by alternating dentils and pendants; grooved, tapered columns with capitals encircled with acanthus leaves; window cornices; recessed front doors with transom and floor-length side lights of Bohemian glass; pilasters; and balcony and porch detail of decorative iron.

Like the exterior, Oakleigh has many architectural features on the inside that were not incorporated into all houses: the fine millwork (Photo), marble mantels, decorative plaster cornices and medallions and the graceful curved stairway with a walnut hand rail. An unusual feature of the floor plan is an oval dining room behind the central

Oakleigh

Oakleigh — curved stairway

Oakleigh — detail of millwork and plasterwork

hallway. Instead of corners, the room has recessed niches for china. The baseboards in the room are wood painted to simulate marble — a fad during the Greek Revival era. Evidently Judge Clapp, who served in the state legislature and was a trustee for the University of Mississippi, appreciated some of the finer things in life.

MONTROSE

Montrose looks like a reflection across the street from Oakleigh. However, the facade detail was simplified and the oval dining room was deleted from the floorplan. Double parlors are located to the left; bedroom and dining room, to the right. These rooms are separated by a central hallway with a beautiful parquet floor (Photo) and a curved stairway that rises at the end of the hallway. The detached kitchen is behind the house.

The house was built by Alfred Brooks, a landowner-planter, as a wedding gift for his daughter, Margaret, when she married Robert McGowan. The house has had many owners, with the city of Holly

Montrose — parquet floor in entrance hall

Montrose

Springs being the present owner. The city leases the house to the Holly Springs Garden Club. The house and furnishings were given to the city by the family of Mrs. Jack Johnson. Mrs. Johnson was the widow of shoe magnate Jack Johnson of St. Louis (both were originally from Holly Springs and were related to the Oscar Johnsons, owners of Walter Place).

WALTER PLACE

When Harvey Washington Walter — former teacher, well-known lawyer and businessman, and a recognized city leader — got ready to build his new house, he was not content to build just another Oakleigh or Montrose. He wanted something that would be distinctive. Therefore, his house plans included the addition of two-story, battle-mented octagonal towers to a classic structure fronted with Corinthian columns. Not only were the towers different but they also provided extra floor space, which the Walters needed for their ten children. The Gothic towers were an asset in later years when three of the rooms were converted into bath-dressing rooms, while the fourth was used as a library.

The house is truly a mansion, with each of its spacious rooms decorated with fine millwork and a marble mantel. These costly features were usually confined to the parlors or public rooms in most houses. (Photo)

The house has two stairways, with the central hallway containing a lovely curved stairway. The second stairway, located between two bedrooms on the second floor, leads to the attic and a secret room in the top of the left tower.

Colonel Walter and his three sons died during the yellow fever epidemic in 1878. The daughters had various interests, among them writing (Minnie), medicine (Annie became a medical missionary to China), and business (Irene married Oscar Johnson of Red Banks, who became head of one of the largest shoe manufacturing companies in the world).

After Mrs. Walter's death, the house was purchased from the estate by Oscar Johnson. The Johnsons lived in St. Louis but maintained Walter Place as a second home. Johnson intensified the beauty of

Walter Place — mantel in parlor featuring Minerva head

Walter Place

Walter Place by transforming the setting into a twenty-acre park. To accomplish this work, a creeping gully behind the house was filled and a skilled architect was hired to design the park. Mr. Kiern, a German landscape architect who was associated with Tower Grove Park in St. Louis, was given the assignment. Trees were imported, formal gardens were established, a swimming pool was constructed, and a local gardener was trained for maintenance work.

To update the house, Theodore C. Link, a noted St. Louis architect who designed the new Mississippi State Capitol, was employed. He changed the stairway to a "welcoming-arms" type, used the tower rooms and part of two bedrooms to make five bathrooms, and planned a utility room and kitchen. The red stained-glass sidelights around the front door were changed to white satin glass with a grape design. Link and Kiern also restored and landscaped some smaller houses on the property to be used as guests houses.

When Mr. Johnson died, Mrs. Johnson sold the house. Ten years later, however, the house was again purchased by Mrs. Oscar Johnson, who had been encouraged by her sister in China, Annie, to buy the home place. The mansion was bought at a courthouse auction for $4,000. At this time, Mrs. Johnson changed the stairway to look like the original.

Mrs. Johnson left the house to her two sons and one daughter. The daughter sold her share to the two brothers. (She purchased and renovated Mosswood.) Since the owners live in St. Louis, the house continues to be used for brief periods. However, the house is cleaned weekly whether it has been occupied or not.

Walter Place is opened annually for the Holly Springs pilgrimage. The house is always a crowd pleaser because of its unusual architectural features, its family and war history (the house was occupied by Mrs. U. S. Grant in 1862), and its interesting furnishings. The furnishings are not the original but are fine pieces collected by the Johnsons. Many of the accessories are oriental objects of art that were selected by Annie Walters in China.

Cedarhurst and Airliewood are both located on Salem Avenue and were constructed of brick in the late 1850s. The houses incorporate features promoted by A. J. Downing in his books concerned with appropriate architecture and landscaping for country houses. Downing considered the Tudor Gothic style ". . . to be the most convenient and comfortable, and decidedly the most picturesque and striking style, for country residences of a superior class."[29] Evidently General U. S. Grant thought the houses to be of superior class also because when he came to Holly Springs in 1862 he selected Airliewood for his headquarters, Cedarhurst for General Ord and Walter Place for Mrs. Grant.

Cedarhurst and Airliewood are picturesque, with their high-pitched roofs broken by decorative gables that are embellished with fanciful bargeboards and accented with finials and pendants. The tall, paired, octagonal chimneys are considered a major part of the Gothic design and are a sharp contrast to the simple chimneys of Greek Revival houses.

The repetition of the pointed arch in the fenestrations underscores the fact that the houses are Gothic. The pointed arch is achieved in Cedarhurst by shaped bricks whereas labels or hoods emphasize the pointed arch on Airliewood. According to Downing ". . . the windows, in the best Tudor mansions, affect a great variety of forms and sizes."[30] Both Cedarhurst and Airliewood meet this qualification as they have single, double, and bay windows. The front windows on the principal floor extend to the floor.

CEDARHURST

In addition to the Gothic features already mentioned, Cedarhurst is trimmed with octagonal colonettes, pointed-arch tracery, and a balustrade — all cast by the local antebellum industry — the Jones,

Cedarhurst

McIlwaine, and Company foundry. The tall trees of holly, cedar and other varieties are in harmony with the vertical lines of the building.

Cedarhurst was built for Dr. Charles Bonner, a Pennsylvanian of Irish decent who married Mary Wilson of Holly Springs. The house is frequently referred to as the home of Sherwood Bonner, the second child of the Charles Bonners, who became a writer of southern dialect stories and secretary to American poet Henry Wadsworth Longfellow.

Catherine Sherwood Bonner had strong feelings for her home place. She frequently referred to the house in her correspondence with Longfellow.[31] On August 31, 1877, she wrote from Holly Springs to Henry Wadsworth Longfellow in Cambridge, Mass.:

> Did I ever tell you what a beautiful home mine was? The place is not well-kept up now, but nothing can take away the grandeur of the old trees, or make the flowers less fragrant. The wide gallery in front is all over run with Madeira vine; it is in full blossom now, and we sit out on the porch every evening in the moonlight, talking of the past days that its aromatic sweetness, more than anything else seems to recall.

Sherwood Bonner returned to Holly Springs to care for her father and brother who died on September 9, 1878 during the yellow fever epidemic. In November, 1878, Miss Bonner wrote to Longfellow concerning cleaning the house after the epidemic: "You know all the carpets have to be taken up, the rooms fumigated, the walls calcimined, and everything thoroughly aired. It is an immense undertaking." In the same letter she wrote: "I do not know what I shall do. There is some talk of a division of property. I know that my father would wish that I should keep the home we love so well; yet I know I should be

Cedarhurst — shaped brick detail

167

so unhappy here, shut in with sorrow; and it is so large a house for only Aunty, Lilian and myself. I cannot *bear* to give it up; and yet I want a home in Boston." In December she wrote: "I had hoped to leave Holly Springs before Xmas; but I am detained here by business matters. It breaks my heart afresh to be here at the time that has never failed of happiness, in the home that always threw open its hospitable doors to welcome Christmas guests." On April 18, 1879: "We are all here together in the old home. Aunty has made up her mind that she cannot live away from it, so she will stay here for the present, at least."

By August 7, 1881, Sherwood Bonner was faced with the possibility of having to sell her home at a public auction if she did not pay her brother-in-law $1500 for her sister's share of the house. She wrote to Mr. Longfellow:

> It is *cruel*. But he is *determined* — Of course it will be sold at an utter sacrifice — as things always are at a forced sale — and we must see this beautiful home go. For myself I would be reckless enough to make no effort to save it — but there is Aunty's old age and Lilian's future to be considered. All the cares of the world seem to crowd upon me — and I am alone. My attorney strongly advises me to close with his offer — saying it is absolutely securing me at a small sum a very fine and valuable property — and that he can borrow the money for me for a long term of years. But you may imagine how I *shrink* from incurring such a debt. I should have to mortgage my part of the plantation — and in case of my death it would be sold. And this is where our only income comes from. The house is nothing but a white elephant. I have asked time to consider and I lay the matter before you, because I know you will help me to some extent. If I could pay them a certain part of the sum, I should be willing to borrow a smaller sum. I shall have three hundred dollars in a week or so, from the Lippincott's — so there is a beginning. And I am trying as well as I can, for the pertubation of my soul, to complete a Harper story, that ought to fetch one hundred more — And you will help me, will you not to save my home — to secure for myself a *retreat* for my ruined life where I may die with dignity . . .

Mr. Longfellow wrote that he would send the money after the middle of the month. He died before fulfilling his promise; however, Miss Alice Longfellow, his daughter, sent the "generous gift" to Miss Bonner.

Sherwood Bonner died of cancer in Holly Springs on July 22, 1883. Her daughter Lilian sold the house around the turn of the century to Mr. W. A. Belk. Cedarhurst is now owned and occupied by Mrs. Fred M. Belk, Sr.

AIRLIEWOOD

Airliewood, built by planter William Henry Coxe, looks different from Cedarhurst because it has been stuccoed, painted a salmon pink, and has a crenelated roof over the verandah instead of the ornamental ironwork. However, the basic form of the exteriors is essentially the same. The battlement design of the Airliewood porch roof is not original, but it is appropriate.

The pointed arch is repeated in the interior millwork of Airliewood. Marble mantels, silver doorknobs, a carved walnut staircase and the park-like setting lend elegance to the structure. The house and setting are enclosed by an iron fence with massive iron gates that were cast

Airliewood — massive iron gates accent entry

Airliewood

by the local foundry. The house is beautifully maintained by its owners Mrs. Charles N. Dean, Sr., and her son, Mr. Charles Dean.

There are other houses in Mississippi that may be considered Gothic, but Cedarhurst and Airliewood are probably the best examples of Gothic mansions in the state.

GRAY GABLES

Gray Gables was originally a small two-story structure that was built by Mariah Nelson, a merchant. In later years the house was purchased by James J. House, who changed the structure from a simple cottage to an ornate Italianate edifice employing rounded arches, wooden tracery spandrels, a decorative balustrade, and brackets. The use of window caps over the front windows was a popular local decoration. The front doorway is a thing of beauty with its arched millwork fitted with deeply cut Bohemian glass (Photo: The darker panes are the original glass).

The house has several interesting interior architectural features. A curved stairway fits the rounded walls at the rear of the entrance hall (Photo). The door under the stairway opens into an oval dining room. The kitchen was attached via a breezeway.

The woodwork design in the parlor is especially noteworthy. A twisted rope design connects carved squares of a small boy on a swan. The traditional story associated with the woodwork is that the owner had this design created in memory of his son who drowned in a lily pond in the yard. He got the idea from the Greek mythological story of Icarus, the adventuresome boy who flew too close to the sun with his wings of wax and fell into the ocean and drowned.

Local history claims that Gray Gables had the first stationary bathtub. Water was provided for the cypress and lead container from a reservoir built into the attic. The water was pumped from a cistern.

Gray Gables — curved stairway

Gray Gables

Gray Gables — deeply etched Bohemian glass

The house has solid brick walls, with each wall extending to the ground. The exterior is stuccoed. The house was restored in the 1950s by the Holly Springs Garden Club. Gray Gables is presently the home of Mr. and Mrs. Fred Swaney.

NOTES TO PART FOUR

1. Dr. William Lowndes Lipscomb, *A History of Columbus, Mississippi during the Nineteenth Century* (Birmingham, Ala.: Press of Dispatch Printing Company, 1909), p. 59.

2. Parochial Reports of May, 1877, Journal of the Diocese, p. 52.

3. Edwina Dakin Williams, *Remember Me to Tom* (New York: G. P. Putnam's Sons, 1963), p. 16.

4. Lipscomb, p. 126.

5. Talbot Hamlin, *Greek Revival Architecture in America* (Oxford University Press, 1944), p. 127.

6. Andrew J. Downing, *A Treatise on the Theory and Practice of Landscape Gardening Adapted to North America with a View to the Improvement of Country Residences . . . with Remarks on Rural Architecture* (New York: C. M. Saxton and Company 1857), p. 118.

7. Reuben Davis, *Recollections of Mississippi and Mississippians* (New York: Houghton-Mifflin and Co. 1890), p. 262.

8. Lipscomb, p. 65.

9. *Ibid.*, p. 66.

10. J. Frazer Smith, *White Pillars* (New York: Bramhall House), p. 93.

11. Personal Interview, Mrs. Robert Snow.

12. Personal Interview, Mr. John Rodabough, Aberdeen Historian.

13. Reuben Davis, p. 270.

14. Samuel Longfellow, editor, *Life of Longfellow* (Boston: Ticknor & Co., 1886), p. 301.

15. Warren G. French, "Joseph Holt Ingraham, Southern Romancer, 1809-1860" (M.A. thesis, University of Texas, 1948), p. 17.

16. *Ibid.*, p. 27.

17. Personal Interview, Mr. John Rodabough, Aberdeen Historian.

18. Charles Moore, *Daniel H. Burnham—Architect Planner of Cities* (New York: Houghton Mifflin Co., 1921), p. 207.

NOTES TO PART FOUR

19. *The Aberdeen Weekly*, May 24, 1912, Vol. 36, no. 47, p. 1.

20. W. D. McCain, *Journal of Mississippi History*, Vol. VIII (1946), pp. 113, 117.

21. Lucein B. Howry, *History of the Howry House* (Oxford, Miss., 1922).

22. Florence E. Campbell, "Journal of the Minutes of the Board of Trustees of the University of Mississippi 1845—1860," (M.A. thesis, University of Mississippi, 1939), p. 41.

23. *Ibid.*

24. A. J. Downing, *The Architecture of Country Houses* (New York: Da Capo Press, 1968), p. 380.

25. Calvert Vaux, "Hints for Country House Builders," *Harpers New Monthly*, Nov., 1855, Vol. II, no. 66, pp. 763-778.

26. Calvert Vaux, *Villas and Cottages* (New York: Harper and Brothers, 1857), p. 312.

27. Andrew Jackson Downing, *Cottage Residences; or A Series of Designs for Rural Cottages and Cottage Villas, and their Gardens and Grounds Adapted to North America* (New York: John Wiley, 1853), p. 148.

28. William B. Hamilton, "Holly Springs, Mississippi to the Year 1878," (M.A. thesis, University of Mississippi, 1931), p. 2.

29. Andrew J. Downing, *A Treatise on the Theory and Practice of Landscape Gardening Adapted to North America with a View to the Improvement of Country Residences . . . op. cit.*, pp. 400, 401.

30. *Ibid.*, 398.

31. Jean Nosser Biglane, "An Annotated and Indexed Edtion of the Letters of Sherwood Bonner (Catherine Sherwood Bonner McDowell), (M.A. thesis, Mississippi State University, 1972).

PART FIVE

Horn Lake
Carrollton
Washington County

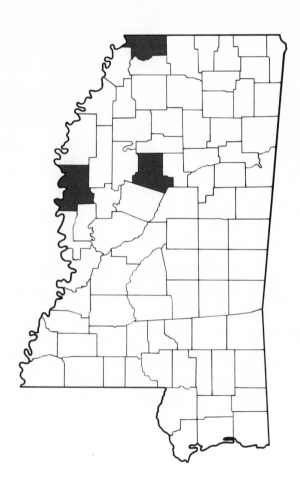

Horn Lake

MON AMOUR

One of the most interesting cottages in the state is Mon Amour, a mid-nineteenth-century octagonal structure built for Dr. William Nathanial Raines and beautifully restored in the early 1970s by Mr. Bryan L. "Bo" Swilley. The house is significant because of its age, shape, construction, source of design, and original owner.

Dr. Raines was a Virginian who came to the Memphis-Horn Lake area to study medicine under Dr. Eldridge. Raines not only acquired medical knowledge from the doctor, he also acquired Eldridge's daughter for his bride.[1] Since Raines was a medical doctor he was probably familiar with the writings of Orson S. Fowler (1809-1887) a phrenologist who became interested in the shapes of houses when he started planning his own home. In the preface of this book *A Home For All* (1854 ed.) Fowler stated that he had briefly turned aside from phrenology "to build him a good home, and in doing so, had made and learned improvements to adopt which will greatly increase home comforts; . . ."[2]

Fowler extolled the octagon form as the ideal shape for a convenient and inexpensive house, and gave his reasons. It encloses one-fifth more space for its walls than the square and is more compact and available. It is easier for the housekeeper to maintain. It is easier to heat and cool. It is easier to entertain large groups and promote sociability. It is easier to incorporate the kitchen (which he calls the stomach of the house) into the main house and thus save almost one-fourth of the net total cost of the whole house. It is easier to sit with your feet to the fire and your back to the window, which is just the thing for reading. It is better to light the room with one large window rather than two or three cross lights, "which confuse and injure the eye, shine through a newspaper and blur it from one window, as you hold it up to read by another, and are every way objectionable, as all opticians assert, and the laws of optics prove." It is more attractive with a dome roof rather than "a cottage roof, full of sharp peaks, sticking out in various directions."[3]

After presenting and defending the virtues of the octagonal form for domestic houses, Fowler then presents several floor plans. The Howland octagonal plan, designed by Messrs. Morgan and Brothers, architects, Williamsburg, New York, for Mr. William Howland, engraver for Fowler's book,[4] is probably the source for the design of the Raines house at Horn Lake, Mississippi (Photo of floor plan in Fowler's book and photo of Raines House).

The exterior elevation and floor plan of the Howland octagonal plan (and essentially the Raines house) are illustrated on pages preceding the title page of Fowler's 1854 edition of *A Home For All* and are illustrated again on pages 110, 111, 112 of the text. The

Mon Amour

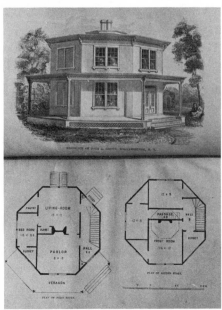

Howland Plan

carpenter's and mason's specifications for the materials and workmanship required to erect and finish a two-story dwelling following the Howland plan for Mr. John J. Brown at East Williamsburg, Long Island, accompany the illustrations (pp. 108–15). Since the elevation, floor plans, and specifications are rather explicit, it would be easy to duplicate the house. According to Fowler, the design was "admired by builders for its neatness, simplicity, convenient arrangement and cheapness."[5] The combination of these factors may have been enough to convince Raines to build the house on some acreage he had acquired from a Mrs. Green at Horn Lake.

It would be interesting to know how many houses in the United States are built following the Howland octagonal plan. The Edward Elderkin house in Elkhorn, Wisconsin, has been described as a "mirror-image of 'Howland's Octagonal Plan'."[6] In addition to the Elkhorn house, Carl Schmidt (who has studied the octagon fad in the United States and Canada) lists the following houses as having the same floorplan as the Howland octagonal plan: Lindsley house in Oxford, New York; the Prime-Klaber house in Huntington, New York; a house in Schobari, New York; and the Groton-Darrow-White house in Kinsman, Ohio.[7] His list did not include Mon Amour.

The Howland plan is a very functional plan that allowed the Raines house to be adapted easily for twentieth-century living. The rooms are not pie-shaped as might be suspected. Instead, there are two large, almost rectangular rooms per floor in the central part of the house with trapazoid rooms on each side to form the octagonal shape (see floor plan). The entrance hall and stairwell are located in the right side of the angular structure. A looping stairway rises from the basement and extends to the second or top story. A small rectangular room and two triangular rooms were located on each level of the left side of the building.

Originally the kitchen, dining room and storage rooms were in the basement while double parlors were on the main floor and the bedrooms were on the second floor. An observatory capped the roof. The plan was adapted in the 1970s by using the lower floor for an office, leisure room, bathroom, storage rooms and air-conditioning system; the second level contains the living room, dining room, and kitchen in the angular room; two bedrooms, two bathrooms and a sitting area are on the upper level.

The Raines house, now known as Mon Amour, is probably sturdier (it now has steel beams) and more attractive than it ever was. This came about because the house happened to be on sixty acres of property that Mr. Bryan Swilley purchased. The eight-sided structure had been unoccupied for some time and the interior had been stripped of any embellishment (except for one mantel and some Ionic capitols in the basement). After consulting with several architects and historians, Mr. Swilley decided to save the house rather than demolish it.

Bryan L. Swilley

Mon Amour — board wall construction

To begin the restoration of the dilapidated house, the exterior and interior wall finishes were removed. This revealed that the house was not a conventional frame building but incorporated the board wall plan that Orson Fowler promoted.[8] For the board wall construction, one-by-four-inch boards were stacked (see illustration) alternating the boards, in an inch and out an inch, thus forming openings for the plaster to clench and eliminating the need for lathing. The boards were anchored with nails driven through each board every three to five feet. Fowler declared this method to be cheaper, warmer, more vermin-proof and to require less time and skill to erect than a frame construction.

The exterior of Mon Amour has been altered twice. Originally it followed the Howland plan; however, the columns may have been ornamented with Ionic capitals. The Ionic capitals, the dentils, and the doorway arrangement would have been carryovers of the Greek Revival style that was the current rage elsewhere in Mississippi. Ionic capitals were found in the basement by Mr. Swilley. These were used to ornament the angled corners of the living room and dining room for the recent renovation.

In 1903 the house was updated by Mr. W. W. Hutchinson who added a porch all around the house. Slender posts with decorative brackets were employed to support the porch roof. In the 1970 restoration a paved brick walk at ground level was substituted for the raised, wooden porch floor. The raised porch was eliminated so that more natural light would penetrate the basement windows. Well-proportioned octagonal columns took the place of the Victorian posts.

The exact date of when the observatory disappeared from the roof is not known. A captain's walk around the central chimney ornaments the roof today. The central chimney has six openings — two per floor. The mantel downstairs is the only original mantel (see Photo). The design of the mantel corresponds with plate number eighty-seven in Minard Lafever's design book *The Modern Builder's Guide,* published in 1833. It, like much of the house, is constructed of yellow poplar.

Mr. William Gwin supervised the original construction of the house.[9] Members of his family had the plans for Mon Amour until recent years. Mr. Roy Mundy supervised the restoration of the house and located exquisite furnishings. A semi-retired carpenter executed the fine interior woodwork. The restoration project required two years to complete.

The mid-nineteenth-century octagonal cottage is situated in the midst of sixty acres of rolling pasture land that insulates the house from twentieth-century suburbia. A small lake, magnolia trees, and brick columns supporting decorative iron gates add to the beauty of Mon Amour.

Mr. Swilley said the restoration of the house cost three times as much as the original estimate, but he is glad he finished the project. Mississippians should be glad, too, that the house was saved because the structure is unique in the state: Longwood in Natchez is an octagonal mansion, the Sullivan cottage at Ocean Springs is a one-story octagonal vacation house, and Mon Amour is a three-level octagonal cottage. In addition, the house is located in an area where historic landmarks are scarce.

Mon Amour — mantel detail

Carrollton

In 1833 Carroll County was established in an area that had belonged to the Choctaw Indians. The town of Carrollton, incorporated two years later, is located on rolling hills at the edge of the Delta, making it a desirable place for planters to live.

The styles of the houses in Carrollton are similar to those in Oxford and Columbus with the mansions (Cotesworth and Malmaison) being two-story wooden structures without architectural orders. Cottages are more plentiful, and, like the cottages in Columbus, many are decorated with brackets, ornamental posts, and wooden spandrels. Stanhope, Helm House, and the Ray home are three fine cottages in Carrollton that are attributed to architect James Clark Harris, who is known primarily for his design of Malmaison for Greenwood Leflore, Choctaw Chieftain. Malmaison (destroyed by fire) was definitely a mansion, but, like the cottages, was ornamented with brackets.

Since at least six buildings in the small town of Carrollton have been attributed to Harris, the architect was instrumental in establishing the picturesque appearance of the small town. Unlike many historic areas in the United States, Carrollton has not been restored — it has been beautifully maintained.

When a film crew was searching for a turn-of-the-century location to film a movie based on William Faulkner's novel *The Reivers*, Carrollton was selected. It was said ". . . the film company had little to do other than cover the streets with sand and build a false front around one service station to create an atmosphere of seventy years ago."[10]

There are numerous historic markers erected in the Carroll County vicinity that refer to the site of Malmaison, the home of Choctaw Chief Greenwood Leflore. The house was destroyed by fire but the site is a historic landmark because of the importance of Leflore.

MALMAISON

Greenwood Leflore was the son of the French trader Louis Lefleur and Rebecca Crevat, niece of Choctaw Chief Pushmataha. In 1824 Greenwood Leflore was elected chief of the Choctaws. He supported the sale of the Choctaw lands to the United States but had the agreement amended whereby any Choctaw desiring to remain in the state would receive a section of land and protection from the government. Leflore remained in Carroll County and became a large cotton planter and a statesman. By mid-nineteenth century he had amassed a fortune. He secured the services of architect James Clark Harris (who later became his son-in-law) to plan a mansion for him.

The large-scale house had two stories with four porticos and an attached wing (see Photos). Decorative brackets, pilasters, iron balconies, and a cupola that afforded a view of the surrounding area ornamented the house.

Malmaison—destroyed by fire (HABS)

Malmaison -– view of porticos (HABS)

The interior featured cross halls with heavy millwork (Photo). According to local history the furnishings, including hand-painted window shades and an aubusson carpet in the parlor, were imported from France.

Leflore's leadership was recognized by the non-Indian population also. He was elected to serve terms in both the state house of representatives and the senate. Leflore was independent and steadfast in his beliefs. During the War Between the States the United States flag flew over Malmaison.[11]

COTESWORTH

Cotesworth was the home of another important Mississippi statesman, J. Z. George, who was instrumental in framing the constitution of Mississippi. The senator was a lawyer who maintained an office to the left of the Carroll County Courthouse. The office is now used as the headquarters for the Carrollton Pilgrimage.

According to family history, Cotesworth was initially an inn located on the stagecoach line to Grenada. Senator George purchased the property in 1847 and enlarged the structure to meet the needs of his family of nine children. He named the house for his friend Judge Cotesworth P. Smith.

Cotesworth, like many houses built in the South, is a two-story building fronted with tall columns. The facade is ornamented with dentils on the cornice and above the windows and doors. The double-hung windows on the first floor are floor length. Decorative iron grillwork outlines the cantilevered balcony.

Entry into the wide central hallway is through double doors framed with side lights and pilasters. A simple stairway rises from the right side of the hall to lead to four bedrooms upstairs. Large parlors are

James Butters

Malmaison — interior (HABS)

Cotesworth

Cotesworth — library

Cotesworth — Senator J. Z. George's library interior. Wooden mantel has been painted to simulate marble.

located on opposite sides of the first-floor hallway. Behind the parlors are smaller rooms with the dining room on the left and a bedroom on the right. A back gallery spans the house and connects with a short breezeway to the kitchen.

On the right side of the house is another breezeway that connects the main house to a room with galleries that was built by Senator George for an office. The office proved to be too accessible to the family; consequently in 1860 he built the hexagon-shaped law library a short distance from the house (Photo).

There are at least three octagonal buildings in the state (Longwood in Natchez; Sullivan Cottage in Ocean Springs; Mon Amour in Horn Lake), but this is the only hexagonal building that the author knows about in the state. The interior (Photo) has a marbelized mantel on the wall opposite the entry. Windows are located on each side of the fireplace. Additional light is obtained from single windows on four sides, a half-glass door on the sixth side, and six windows in the dome. A bookshelf originates from each of the six corners and advances toward the center of the room. The area under the dome is left open. The boards for the floor in this area are laid to repeat the hexagonal shape.

The source for the design of this building is not known. Orson S. Fowler and Samuel Sloan had published articles and design books advocating the octagonal form for houses, and Andrew J. Downing had included a hexagonal gate house in one of his publications. These writings advocating the angular form for buildings had been very popular the decade immediately preceding the construction of the law library. The paired brackets and the decorative posts are similar to those on buildings in the vicinity that are attributed to architect James Clark Harris.

Senator George left Cotesworth to his son, W. C. George, with the stipulation that it be left with someone in good standing in the Baptist Church. W. C. George left the house to his sister, Mrs. Lizzie George Henderson, who in time left the house to her brother, Mr. J. W. George, who was the father and grandfather of the present owners. For a number of years the house was left furnished but unoccupied. The house and office were never broken into.

The present owners (Mrs. M. P. Saunders and Mr. and Mrs. J. B. Williams, Jr.) expanded the house by adding a kitchen and family room to the rear of the original kitchen. The house is now a big, rambling, comfortable home with a variety of galleries, balconies, breezeways, and patios where one can sit and enjoy the beauty of nature on the surrounding acreage.

Washington County

Antebellum structures in the Delta are few since this area was plagued with floods until levees were constructed. The Delta area south of Greenville near Lake Washington was settled first by Kentuckians: Junius Ward, Henry Johnson, and four Worthington brothers. These landowners eventually built fine houses. Fire and floods destroyed most of them, but two fine Italianate mansions still exist to give us some indication of life in the Delta before 1860.

BELMONT

The site where William Worthington decided to build his mansion belonged to his brother Samuel. In earlier years the land had belonged to Alexander G. McNutt, a Mississippi governor. William acquired the site and had a building constructed that is more Italianate than Classic, with its decorative spandrels forming arches between the columns and with its many brackets under the eaves. The interior millwork and plasterwork incorporate Greek motifs.

The main block of the red brick structure contains eight rooms divided by central hallways. A stairway rises from the left rear of the hall and crosses to the right. The windows on the front part of the house are floor length to open onto the galleries. The eleven-foot doorway is framed with etched and stained side lights (five rectangular panes on each side that come to the floor) and transom lights. The ceilings in the parlor, central hall, and dining room are lavishly embellished with intricate plaster designs.

An ell is attached to the right rear of the house, thus making the right side six rooms deep. As in Riverview in Columbus, pilasters are located between the windows, creating a pattern on the lengthy wall.

Belmont

The right side of the house had double parlors that could be divided by sliding doors. The past tense is used here because the house is now the property of a hunting club and the use of the rooms has changed since the house was constructed around 1857. Behind the parlors (in the ell) was the dining room, kitchen, butler's pantry, stair-hall, and bedroom. Additional bedrooms were on the second level of the house and ell.

Behind the house are old cisterns and two brick buildings probably used for the smokehouse (for meat) and the dairy (to cool dairy products).

MOUNT HOLLY

Mount Holly is a spacious Italianate mansion that was started in 1853 and completed except for minor elements in 1859 for Margaret Johnson Erwin. Mrs. Erwin was the daughter of Henry Johnson, one of several Kentuckians to first settle permanently in the Lake Washington area.

Mount Holly

Mount Holly — note shaped bricks in arches and column

Mount Holly — service buildings

Mount Holly — bricks molded to fit angles at corners

Margaret Johnson married James Erwin (whose first wife had been Henry Clay's only daughter, Anne Brown).

The rounded arches, bay windows, asymmetrical plan, brackets, balconies and projecting central facade are the pronounced features of the house and indicate its style—Italianate. Ammadelle in Oxford contains many of the same features. In fact, the floor plan for Mount Holly follows very closely to design number twenty-seven in Calvert Vaux's *Cottages and Villas* (the source for the design of Ammadelle) if the left side of the house were switched to the right side. Mrs. Erwin's great grandson maintains that the house was designed by Samuel Sloan — the architect from Philadelphia who designed Longwood in Natchez. Letters to support this statement, however, cannot be located. Regardless of who designed Mount Holly, it is a lovely structure.

Mount Holly is constructed of bricks molded in various sizes and shapes to meet specific purposes. Note the shaped bricks in the columns, the bay windows and the arched windows (Photo).

Entry is into a spacious hallway with niches for statuary. The stairway is in a hall to the right rear of the entry hall. The floor plan includes parlors, a dining room, library, conservatory, pantry, kitchen and two bedrooms on the principal floor; a ballroom, music room and additional bedrooms on the second level. Four porches and service buildings are attached to the house. The spacious villa overlooks Lake Washington and was the center of social life in Washington County for many years.

NOTES TO PART FIVE

1. Thomas E. Michael, "The Eight-Sided House", *Mid-South Magazine*, Memphis, Tenn., May 30, 1965.
2. Orson S. Fowler, *A Home for All* (New York: Fowler and Wells, 1854), p. iii.
3. *Ibid.*, pp. 82-103.
4. *Ibid.*, p. 108.

5. *Ibid.*, p. 108.

6. Walter Creese, "Fowler and the Domestic Octagon," *Art Bulletin,* Vol. 28, no. 2, p. 100.

7. Carl Schmidt, *The Octagon Fad* (Scottsville, New York, 1958).

8. Fowler, pp. 179, 180.

9. Michael, *op. cit.*

10. Greenwood-Leflore County Chamber of Commerce, *A Tourist Guide to History in Carroll and Leflore Counties, Mississippi* (Greenwood, Miss. 1969), p. 13.

11. Federal Writers Project, *Mississippi: A Guide to the Magnolia State* (New York: Viking Press, 1938), p. 404.

Appendix

LIST OF BUILDINGS, HOME OWNERS AND ADDRESSES

ABERDEEN

Dunlee	Mrs. Virginia Sykes	301 High Street
First Methodist Church	——	
Holliday Haven	Mrs. Carolyn Evans Sauter	South Meridian Street
Masonic Temple	Masons	North Meridian Street
Old Homestead	Mr. and Mrs. Julian Evans, Jr.	Commerce Street
St. John's Episcopal Church		Commerce Street
Sunset Hill	Mr. and Mrs. W. Emerson Jones	Commerce Street
The Magnolias	Mrs. James Acker	Commerce Street
Lenoir Plantation	Mr. and Mrs. Whitman H. Lenoir	Prairie, Highway 45

BILOXI

Beauvoir	United Sons of Confederate Veterans (Mississippi Division)	Highway 90
Episcopal Chapel	——	Highway 90
French House	Mrs. Mary Mahoney	138 Magnolia Street
Gillis House	——	Highway 90
Old Brick House	Biloxi Garden Clubs	410 East Bayview Avenue
Ralph Wood House	Mrs. Ralph Wood	523 East Beach
Spanish House	Mr. and Mrs. Joseph Collins	206 West Water Street
Woodlawn	Mrs. Garner H. Tullis	947 East Beach

CANTON

Grace Episcopal Church	——	Mississippi Highway 16
Madison County Courthouse	——	Courthouse Square
Mosby House	Mr. and Mrs. W. J. Mosby	Center Street
Shackleford House	Mr. and Mrs. B. C. Shackleford	Mississippi Highway 16

CARROLLTON

Cotesworth	Mr. and Mrs. J. B. Williams, Jr., and Mrs. M. P. Saunders	Carrollton
Senator J. Z. George's Library		Carrollton

COLUMBUS

Amzi Love	Mrs. Edith Woodward	305 South Seventh Street
Annunciation Catholic Church	——	808 South Second Avenue
Camellia Place	Mr. and Mrs. John M. Kaye	416 North Seventh Street
Colonnade	Dr. and Mrs. William Sanders	602 South Second Street
Errolton	Mr. and Mrs. Douglas Bateman	216 South Third Avenue
First Methodist Church	——	602 Main Street
Franklin Square	Mr. and Mrs. W. I. Rosamond	423 North Third Avenue
Homewood	Mrs. Louise Wood Cox	702 Main Street
Lee Home	Lee Home Foundation	Seventh Street North
Lehmquen	Mrs. Augusta Equen Lehmberg	613 South Second Street
Lowndes County Courthouse	——	Second Avenue North
Pratt Thomas Home	Mr. and Mrs. Pratt Thomas	519 South Second Street
Riverview	Dr. and Mrs. John Murfee, Jr.	514 South Second Street
Rosedale	Mr. and Mrs. Powell Fleming	1523 South Ninth Street
St. Paul's Episcopal Church Rectory	——	318 South Second Avenue
Shadowlawn	Mrs. T. A. McGahey	1024 South Second Avenue

Snowdoun	Mrs. Frank Vestal	906 North Third Avenue
Temple Heights	Mr. and Mrs. Carl H. Butler, III	515 North Ninth Street
The Cedars	Mrs. T. Bailey Hardy	Military Road at Billups Drive
Themerlaine	Mr. and Mrs. J. Merle Graham	510 North Seventh Street
Twelve Gables	Mr. and Mrs. W. E. McClure	220 South Third Street
Waverley	Mr. and Mrs. Robert Snow	Columbus vicinity, Highway 50
White Arches	Mr. and Mrs. Ned Hardin	122 South Seventh Avenue
Whitehall	Dr. and Mrs. J. E. Boggess	607 South Third Street

GAUTIER

Oldfields	Mr. Earl McKee	Gautier
Old Place Plantation House	Mr. and Mrs. John Gautier	Highway 90

HOLLY SPRINGS

Airliewood	Mrs. Charles N. Dean, Sr. and Mr. Charles N. Dean	Salem Avenue
Bank of Holly Springs	——	Holly Springs Square
Cedarhurst	Mrs. Fred M. Belk, Sr.	Salem Avenue
Christ Episcopal Church	——	Randolph Street
Crump Place	Mr. and Mrs. Roger Woods	Gholson Avenue
Featherston Place	Mr. and Mrs. Jim B. Buchanan	Craft Street
First Presbyterian Church	——	Memphis Street
Fort Daniel	Mr. and Mrs. Fort Daniel	Memphis Street
Gray Gables	Mr. and Mrs. Fred Swaney	College Avenue
Herndon	Mr. and Mrs. Tom Lacey	Falconer Street
Land Office	Mrs. Lynn Hopson	Gholson Avenue
Latoka	Mrs. Claude B. Smith	Randolph Street
Magnolias	Mrs. Everett Slayden	Craft Street
Maxland	Mrs. M. C. Simpson, Sr.	Salem Avenue
Montrose	City of Holly Springs	Salem Avenue
Mosswood	Mrs. Malcolm Moss	Salem Avenue
Oakleigh	Mr. and Mrs. Glenn Fant	Salem Avenue
Tallaloosa	Mrs. Malcolm Moss	Holly Springs vicinity
The Depot	Dr. and Mrs. R. L. Wyatt	975 Van Dorn
Tuckahoe	Mr. and Mrs. J. Clark Cochran	Craft Street
Walter Place	Mr. and Mrs. Oscar Johnson and Mr. and Mrs. Lee Johnson	West Chulahoma Avenue
Walthall-Freeman	City of Holly Springs	College Avenue
White Pillars	Dr. J. A. Hale	Maury Street

HORN LAKE

Mon Amour	Mr. Bryan L. "Bo" Swilley	Upper Horn Lake Road

JACKSON

Governor's Mansion	State of Mississippi	Capitol Street
Hinds County Courthouse	Hinds County	Raymond, Mississippi
Jackson City Hall	City of Jackson	203 South President Street
Manship House	Mrs. Dudley Phelps	412 Fortification Street
Mississippi State Capitol	State of Mississippi	Mississippi and Congress Streets
Old Mississippi State Capitol	State of Mississippi	State and Capitol Streets
The Oaks	Colonial Dames of America in Mississippi	823 North Jefferson Street

MACON

Belle Oaks	Mr. and Mrs. Julius L. Klaus, Jr.	911 Jefferson Street
Cline House	Sullivan Family	Jefferson Street
Harrison House	Mr. Joe Stevens	Jefferson Street
Flora Residence	Mr. and Mrs. E. G. Flora, Jr.	904 Wayne Street

MANNSDALE

Chapel of the Cross	Episcopal Church	Mississippi Highway 463

APPENDIX

NATCHEZ

Airlie	Ayers P. Merrill Family	Myrtle Avenue
Arlington	Mrs. Anne Gwin Vaughan	East Main Street
Auburn	City of Natchez	Duncan Park
Chamber of Commerce	Natchez-Adams County	Commerce Street
Christ Church		Church Hill
Concord Dependency		——
Connelly's Tavern	Mrs. Emmett Burns	
D'Evereux	Natchez Garden Club	Canal Street
	Mr. and Mrs. T. B. Buckles and	Highway 61 North
	Mr. and Mrs. T. B. Buckles, Jr.	
Dunleith	Mr. and Mrs. N. Leslie Carpenter	Homochitto Street
Edgewood	Mr. and Mrs. Richard A. Campbell	Pine Ridge Community
Elms Court	Mrs. Douglas H. MacNeil	Highway 61 South
Elward	Mrs. Walter P. Abbott	Washington Street
Evansview	The National Society of	107 South Broadway Street
	Colonial Dames of America	
Gloucester	Morrison Family	Lower Woodville Road
Green Leaves	Beltzhoover Family	Rankin Street
Holly Hedges	Mr. Earl Hart Miller	Washington Street
Hope Farm	Mr. and Mrs. J. Balfour Miller	Homochitto Street
King's Tavern	Pilgrimage Garden Club	Jefferson Street
Kingston Methodist Church		Kingston
Leisure House	Mr. and Mrs. Harold Leisure	Wall Street
Linden	Richard Conner Feltus Family	Linden Drive
Longwood	Pilgrimage Garden Club	Lower Woodville Road
Melrose	Mrs. George Malin Davis Kelly	Melrose Avenue
Mistletoe	Mr. Samuel Hopkins Lambdin	Pine Ridge Community
Mount Locust	National Park Service	Natchez Trace
Mount Repose	Mr. and Mrs. Ferd Sessions	Pine Ridge Community
Parsonage	Mr. and Mrs. Orrick Metcalfe	South Broadway Street
Presbyterian Manse	First Presbyterian Church	Rankin Street
Rosalie	Mississippi Society Daughters	100 Orleans Street
	of the American Revolution	
Saragossa	Davidson R. Smith Family	Lower Woodville Road
Springfield	National Park Service	Near Natchez Trace
Stanton Hall	Pilgrimage Garden Club	Pearl and High Streets
Texada	Dr. and Mrs. George W. Moss	Wall Street
The Briars	Mr. and Mrs. Patrick A. McDonough, III	——
The Elms	Mrs. Joseph B. Kellogg	South Pine
The Gardens	Mrs. Fred Davis Gilbert	Cemetery Road
Van Court	Dr. and Mrs. Hall Ratcliffe, Jr.	510 Washington Street
Wigwam	Mr. and Mrs. L. A. White	Oak Street
Williamsburg	Mr. and Mrs. R. Bruce Davis	821 Main Street

OCEAN SPRINGS

Charnley Bungalow	Mr. and Mrs. Edsel Ruddiman	East Beach Drive
Octagonal Cottage	Mr. Bill Ruddiman	East Beach Drive
Sullivan Cottage	Monsignor Gregory R. Kennedy	East Beach Drive
St. John's Episcopal Church	——	——

OXFORD

Ammadelle	Mrs. John F. Tatum	Lamar Avenue
Cedar Oaks	Oxford-Lafayette Historic Homes, Inc.	Murray Avenue
Fiddler's Folly	Mrs. J. E. Elkins	Lamar Avenue
Howry-Wright-Purser	Mrs. F. M. Purser	University Avenue
Isom-Worthy House	Mrs. H. D. Worthy	1003 Jefferson Street
L. Q. C. Lamar House	Mr. and Mrs. Harold Houston	616 North Fourteenth Street
Lyceum Building	University of Mississippi	University of Mississippi
Rowan Oak—William Faulkner's Home	University of Mississippi	University of Mississippi
St. Peter's Episcopal Church	——	——

PASCAGOULA

Frederic House	——	——
Longfellow House	Ingalls Ship Building Corporation	East Beach Boulevard
Spanish Fort	Jackson County Historical Society	North of U. S. 90

PONTOTOC

Lochinvar	Dr. Forrest Tutor	Pontotoc vicinity, Highway 15

PORT GIBSON AND VICINITY

Bethel Presbyterian Church	——	State Road 552
Disharoon House	Mrs. G. L. Disharoon	Church Street
Englesing House	Mrs. Frank C. Englesing	702 Church Street
First Presbyterian Church	——	Church Street
Gage House	Mr. and Mrs. James W. Person	602 Church Street
Idlewild	Mrs. Fannie Eaton	——
Oakland Chapel	Alcorn A & M Campus	Lorman, Mississippi
Planter's Hotel	Dr. J. A. Morris and Dr. W. F. Jackson	Main Street
Rodney Presbyterian Church	Daughters of the Confederacy	Rodney, Mississippi
Sacred Heart Catholic Church	Rodney Foundation, Inc.	Rodney, Mississippi
St. Joseph's Catholic Church	——	Church Street
Windsor Ruins	Magruder Family	State Road 552

SANDY HOOK

John Ford House	Marion County Historical Society	Highway 35

VICKSBURG

Anchuca	Mr. and Mrs. Lombard Burns	First Street
Cedar Grove	Vicksburg Theatre Guild	2200 Oak Street
Duff Green House	Salvation Army	806 Locust Street
McNutt House	Mississippi Historic Foundation of Vicksburg	712 Monroe Street
McRaven	Mr. and Mrs. O. E. Bradway, Jr.	East Harrison Street
Old Courthouse	——	Monroe Street
Plain Gables	Mr. and Mrs. W. McCulloch Childs	Locust Street
Planter's Hall	Vicksburg Council of Garden Clubs, Inc.	822 Main Street
Seargent S. Prentiss Building	Godfrey, Bassett, Pitts, Tuminello, A.I.A.	170 Monroe Street

WASHINGTON

Brandon Hall	Mr. and Mrs. Raymond J. St. Germain	Washington
Jefferson College	State of Mississippi	Washington
Ingleside	J. T., Earl and Aileen Rawlings	Washington

WASHINGTON COUNTY

Belmont	Belmont Lodge, Inc.	Wayside
Mount Holly	Mr. and Mrs. John Cox	Erwin

WILKINSON COUNTY

Cold Spring	Mrs. McGehee Reed	Pinckneyville
John Wall House	Wall Family	Pond
Lewis Home	Mr. and Mrs. Gordon L. Morris	Church Street, Woodville
Salisbury	Sheppard Family	Pond
Rosemont	Mr. Percival Beacroft	One mile east of Woodville

Index